Corporate Culture - Combining Purpose and Values

How a poor culture can stifle creativity, innovation, and success - and how to fix it

By
Nick A. Shepherd

ISBN 978-1-7775703-2-3

Cover design by: EduVision Inc.
Library of Congress Control Number:

Books by the same author
"Variance Analysis for Cost Performance Measurement"
"Governance, Accountability and Sustainable Development: An agenda for the 21st Century"
"The Controllers Handbook" (2nd edition)
"Reflective Leaders & High Performance Organizations" (jointly with Dr. Peter Smyth)
"How Accountants Lost Their Balance"

Dedication

To all the people that I have lived with, rubbed shoulders with and worked with over the years who have taught me about life. Thanks also to all the people in the professional associations, clients and employers in Canada, the UK and beyond, who all added to my learning experiences.

A special thanks to Dr. Peter Smyth who strengthened my belief in the human side of business, and who I worked with for over 25 years, and for his support on our joint book "Reflective Leaders and High-Performance Organizations."

Special thanks to my wife Janet and our extended family Lee, Ted, Ben, Lindsay, and Erin Reeves, David Shepherd and Abbey Vint, and Sarah Shepherd, for their patience and support over the years,

Contents

Foreword

This book represents 50 years of learning, during which a revolution in business has taken place. This revolution has seen a shift to where people have become <u>the</u> critical component in building a sustainable enterprise. Successful organizations have moved from talking about "people as their greatest asset" to making this statement a reality. This has led to a lot of talk about corporate culture.

This book is about corporate culture; what it is, how to understand it and how to create and sustain it. It is not a program. It is not a one-time project.

If you are an investor, board member, leader or manager, these concepts will show how you need to refine your organization in a way that puts people on an equal level of importance to money. Paying people is the often the greatest use of cash, yet for many, much of this money is wasted because people are not motivated to deliver their optimum performance. As a result, your organization suffers, not just from sub-optimum performance but from an increased risk of behavioural surprises.

These ideas come in most cases from actual, practical experience during my career. However, it has been a learning process during which I did a lot of things wrong. It was a journey, because along the way, I gathered different pieces of the puzzle until, later in my career I was able to put the pieces together. By this time, I had left my twenty five years "in corporate" behind me and I was running my own training and consulting business. Many of the ideas were developed and implemented in conjunction with clients who were willing to "try them out." Many of my initial thought were contained in my book "Governance, Accountability and Sustainable Development: An agenda for the 21st century" which was published in 2005 but at that point my learning still had a way to go.

In 2012 Dr. Peter Smyth and I published "Reflective Leaders and High-Performance Organizations" that brought together many of the lessons about human performance and leadership behaviour that we had gained from applying our ideas with clients over many years of working together on team-development and executive support.

This book builds further on these ideas, but also presents a more holistic and integrated approach to organizational strategy. Firstly, there is a lot of talk "out there" about "integrated thinking" and "Integrated reporting." This book looks at integration from an organizational perspective. This includes consideration of ALL stakeholders and the growth of non-financial resources as critical components of value creation. One could say this book is about "making integrated thinking work."

The book is also about sustainability - but sustainability of the enterprise for the benefit of both the owners, who have financial capital at risk, but also for many others in society who benefit from the existence and operation of a well run business. Whilst this incorporates sustainability in its use as a term for ESG or Environment, Social and Economic aspects, there is little point in worrying about this, if an enterprise fails to be itself, sustainable.

This book also complements my 2021 book "How Accountants Lost Their Balance." Business remains heavily committed to reliance upon financial information and reporting as a tool to understand the effective functioning of a business. However, as organizations have transformed to become more human centric, accountants and financial reporting have tracked and reported less of the information necessary to understand the effective functioning of a business. Worse than this, the award of a "clean audit report" and confirmation of an organization as a "going concern" has become an unreliable indicator of business health and continuity.

In the first chapter we will "scope out" the concept of organizational culture; after that we will explain how this approach must start at the highest level with strategy and planning. We then demonstrate how every activity within the organization must be planned, structured, and aligned to ensure a consistent message.

At the end of the book, we include a chapter on the growing importance of tools, to help an organization better understand, coach, and develop people. As organizations become increasingly "people centric" so it will become increasingly critical to understand human personality and behaviour especially in the group context. Human "typing" to fit people into pre-defined boxes is not suggested - however understanding unique human tendencies and responses **is** an important consideration. As the science of understanding develops, so this can be valuable tool.

Nick Shepherd
Ottawa, March 2021

Corporate Culture

1 Executive Summary

I know time is short so here is the essence of this book. There are four important reasons to read this book.

1. To rebuild the credibility of the capitalist business model.
2. To increase profitability and growth.
3. To decrease risk (and cost) of failure from poor control.
4. To protect the drivers of value creation that underpin your business model.

Society has been "falling out" with the world of business for the last thirty years because of perceived primacy of shareholders. In 2019 the CEOs of the Business Roundtable adopted a new Statement on the Purpose of a Corporation declaring that companies should serve not only their shareholders, but also deliver value to their customers, invest in employees, deal fairly with suppliers, and support the communities in which they operate. This replaced a 22-year old focus on shareholder primacy.

This is a good start, but CEO's must shift corporate strategy to provide equal focus on the purpose of the organization and the behaviour of the organization. It is poor behaviour that often drives a poor reputation.

Secondly poor behaviour, often caused by a "less than optimum" corporate culture, is costing money in "surprises" such as penalties and fines from regulators, and hidden excess operating costs. It is also depressing the ability to grow through innovation and creativity. Fix the behaviour, both internally and externally and unleash the human potential for innovation, creativity, communications, and collaboration.

Third, many of the surprises are caused by poor control. While many organizations have adopted Codes of Ethics or Codes of Conduct these fail if they are not embedded in the thoughts and actions at every level of the business. What do employees do when there are no policies or procedures, and they have to decide? Do they know what "corporate values" should drive their decision making? Control failures from Enron to Carillion have shown that leaving people to make their own decisions and relying on a clean audit report means little in a world where value creation is driven by non-financial assets.

Finally, many executives are operating blind. Billions are being poured into the creation of value creating intangible assets. This is not being reported or tracked financially. Audits do not reveal whether these assets are being damaged or depleted. It is the wrong behaviour that often destroys intangibles. Poor behaviour of leaders. Poor behaviour with suppliers, Poor behaviour with customers. All of that money poured into doing the right thing, now wasted because the culture is depleting its value creating ability.

A healthy business in a people centric driven, "asset light" world is all about leadership and behaviour. About Corporate Culture. This book provides some guidance as to how to make it happen.

At the end of each chapter there is a short summary and checklist of the key points.

2 Introduction

CORPORATE CULTURE IS ABOUT "HOW
THINGS ARE DONE AROUND HERE." THE
ENVIRONMENT THAT LEADERS CEATE TO OPTIMZE
THE RESOURCES THEY USE

As human resources have become increasingly important to business performance, so has the challenge for leadership to create an environment where every dollar spent is an investment and not a cost. I remember being asked, some years ago by a major global pharmaceutical company, to attend one of their senior executive meetings and explain what this "thing" called corporate culture really is. Even asking the question was troubling.

There is no right culture. No consulting firm can tell you how to solve your corporate culture "issues." It is like going to a marriage counsellor and asking them to "fix" your marriage. No two relationships are the same because no two people are the same. It is the same in business. Culture is unique to each organization. What makes it REALLY hard is that people are unique, fickle, and different. Many of their actions are driven as emotional responses, no matter how "committed" they are.

But make no mistake; every organization has a culture - even if it has never been defined as such. This is a broad and inclusive area. It is about values and principles; about ethics and beliefs; about hiring approaches and pay principles; it is about communications, collaboration, and cooperation; it is about silos and territorial management; it is about trust, fairness, and transparency. It is also about the underlying approaches to suppliers and customers; to regulators; to investors and owners; to family members. It is about relationships with society and community. It is about how the work gets planned and executed. It is about how direction is given and problems are solved. Everything. That is why it is so hard.

One could use this frightening statement as the foundation for the importance of culture:

AN ORGANIZATION IS NOTHING MORE THAN A
GROUP OF INDIVIDUALS BROUGHT TOGETHER IN
ORDER TO FULFIL A COMMON PURPOSE.

Every one of these people brought together has their own ideas about how the common purpose might be achieved. Some might suggest that the job of the leader is to define both the purpose and how it will be achieved. Others may suggest that rather than telling people how to achieve the purpose, we leave up to them to decide. Both are dangerous.

As seen above, it is about everything that the organization does. Jan Carlzon was the CEO of SAS (Scandinavian Airlines) many years ago, at a time when customer service was an area of competitive focus for the airline industry. He "coined a phrase" that every CEO should think about when considering organizational culture. The phrase was "moments of truth."

A moment of truth occurs every single time there is an interaction, in Jan's case with an SAS employee, and with an existing or potential customer. He made the point that it is this one-on-one experience that reflects what the company is, and what it stands for. If that interaction is positive, that is great for the company; if it is negative the opposite is true.

No number of plaques on the wall, speeches by the CEO or other leaders or corporate messages can create a brand and a reputation. It is done event by event. Day after day after day. There is no program. There is no start or finish. It is just the way you do things. This was the core message in Jim Collins "Good to Great." The challenge, as was demonstrated by the years that have elapsed since his book that "good to great" can happen over time but if you ever lose the culture, everything else starts to fall apart. A new CEO whose "values" are different. An acquisition and integration between two cultures that are different and unique (remember Chrysler merger with Daimler-Benz that ended up costing the shareholders billions?)

Organizational culture is not a new issue or challenge, but it has become more critical. First, people - often referred to as human capital, have *really* become an organizations greatest asset. Do not look for them as an asset on the accounting balance sheet because they are not there (that is another whole issue).

People were always important - in many cases to operate the machines and equipment that drove operational activity. But in many cases, the demand for underlying skills and education were lower; training times were reasonably short and much of the work involved following instructions and escalating problems when they occurred. Employees were also quite easily replaced. Hired in good times and laid off in bad times.

As the knowledge economy grew, more machinery was automated calling for skilled employees to both set up the automation and operate the equipment. Less people could then operate more machines so the number of unskilled or less skilled jobs decreased and the more skilled jobs increased. However, people with skills tend to be more expensive, more mobile, and more independent; they also tend to grow in value to the business, as they learned how to integrate their skills with the needs of the organization and their work.

Any organization, that traditionally worked on the "command and control" approach to management soon found that these more skilled employees could only be retained if it provided a positive working environment (read "culture"). The past approach of looking at employees as an "easily replaceable cost" had to be changed. This started the shift from "personnel management" to "human resources" and then to "talent" management.

It also changed the role of anyone in a supervisory or leadership position who had to adopt a collaborative, coaching, and supporting role aimed at engaging everyone in the goals of the business. Creating an environment where everyone could contribute ideas for improvement that would be taken seriously and not rejected because "they weren't a qualified engineer." This issue of motivation reminds me of a story originally attributed to H. J. Chapman who must have been an engineer. It is called the "Allegorical Goose Farm Fable."

"Once upon a time there were two farmers each of whom had a flock of geese that laid golden eggs. The goodly farmer liked his geese and fed them well. The more the geese produced the better he fed them and improved their farm. The geese that laid the largest eggs were appointed to train others to lay bigger eggs and at the same time they kept on laying eggs themselves. He continued to buy new geese that looked like good layers to add to his flock. So, the farm prospered, and the geese were a happy lot.

Across the valley lived a tyrannical farmer. He was afraid of his geese because he thought that if they revolted and took over the farm, he would starve since he was incapable of producing the eggs himself. So, he treated the geese badly, fed them the least he could, yelled and screamed at them to produce more and chopped off the heads of the best layers whenever they squawked back. He appointed the poorest layers or sterile geese to supervise and ordered them to get more eggs out of the flock. They pecked at the best layers and honked for all the geese to hear. Whenever a goose fought back, they asked the farmer to chop off her head. So, the flock produced less, the eggs got smaller and some flew the coop. The farmer now bought more geese as replacements selecting not the big layers but conformists that would fit into the flock. Finally, conditions got so bad and so many layers escaped that the farmer went bankrupt and lost his farm.

In great anger the tyrannical farmer tore across the valley to the goodly farmer. He told a tale of how he had been so good to his geese and they had taken advantage of him, had revolted, and taken over the farm, that they had held him prisoner and finally stolen all his eggs and absconded with the money leaving him bankrupt. He told the goodly farmer not to make the same mistake but to rule his flock with an iron hand and chop the heads off of any troublemakers.

What the farmer did not understand is that geese never want the farm or to run it; the only want to lay eggs. In society, perhaps the engineers are the geese that lay the golden eggs for the economic welfare of the country and the good of all."

While the story might be overstated it does demonstrate the difference in thinking and about the nature of a "good culture" and how it affects the workforce. In effect leadership at all levels creates the environment within which all aspects of organizational resources can be optimized. Note the use of the word "optimized." A successful organization is all about balance; balance creates sustainability; life, including business, is full of "trade-offs" where one has to give up a bit of one thing to gain something else. A growing criticism of business is that "financial capital is winning and everything else (including the planet) is losing." However, this is an oversimplification.

In a free market, where financial capital moves about, there is always a risk of becoming less attractive to a provider of capital. Therefore, in a well balanced organization, financial performance must remain important - but the impact of trade-off decisions on the other resources, that are critical to value creation must be understood and evaluated. Good leaders do this - but to a degree they have to "fly by the seat of their pants." There is limited information to demonstrate the impact of these decisions. This is especially critical when these trade-off decisions impact people.

Culture starts with strategy and leadership, but leaders will fail unless the commitment to a certain level of behaviour is embedded into the fabric of the whole organization and reinforced task-by-task, interaction-to-interaction. This requires that behavioural expectations share an equal level of importance with corporate purpose - being the mission or vision of the business. This book will show how to make that happen. It sounds easy but it is not as has been proven.

Since the fall of Enron, along with a number of other corporate scandals, US companies have been required to comply with SOX (Sarbanes-Oxley). One of the key aspects of SOX is an assessment of internal controls. The framework for performing this aspect of an annual financial audit, is a risk assessment approach originally developed in 1992, and it starts with an assessment of "the tone at the top." The challenge is that the tone at the top, may appear to be good, but the inability to embed the intent into the corporate fabric often results in unplanned surprises. One only has to look at scandals like the Wells Fargo events of 2016 to see that a company meeting the apparent legislative requirements goes "missing in action."

One of the greatest challenges faced by business is there is not a clear ROI from many of the activities required to create, affirm, and perpetuate an effective culture. It is interesting that looking back, we see this was also the case when many western nations were facing competition from Japan and a core aspect of change was the focus on quality management.

At the time, many organizations thought they understood the issue and were paying for inspectors whose job it was to identify and resolve quality issues. While this was an "overhead cost" it was felt necessary to spend a minimum amount, keep quality problems at an acceptable level. But this was failing. While Japan sought "first time right every time" and designed their organizations to operate that way, many in the western world, felt that a 3% or 5% defect level was acceptable. After all organizations tracked scrap and rework costs as well as customer returns so they knew what the cost was.

Category	Uncertainty	Awakening	Enlightened	Wisdom	Certainty
Characteristics	Minimal or no understanding	Focus on doing better, such as motivational talks	Develop and implement multi stage "holistic" improvement programs	Embedding programs and focus on continuity of improvement	Quality is an embedded value in everything we do
Actual excess costs as a % of sales	~ 20%	~ 18%	~ 12%	~ 8%	~ 2.5%
Reported or known excess costs	0%	3%	8%	6.5%	2.5%

Figure 1 Cost of poor quality - theory to reality

Wrong. The costs at the organizational level were WAY higher than the financial reporting was showing. One of the quality gurus at the time wrote a book, that included a table that organizations could use to figure out where they were in terms of known and unknown poor quality costs.

Using a concept called COPQ or Cost of Poor Quality Philip Crosby demonstrated that for many organizations they "didn't know what they didn't know." The costs of poor quality could be as high as 20% due to hidden costs that were not being tracked. That number did not even include the negative impact of an organizations relationships with its customers or the impact on the total system capacity to earn revenue. Leaders soon discovered that by focusing their whole organization on quality from the design stage to post sales, from operations to administration, they could earn significant returns.

This is where we are today in culture. There is a significant cost to poor culture that includes major risks to an organization. The cost of a poor culture can be assessed in a similar way to the cost of poor quality. For more explanation on this underlying cost of poor quality, there is a study on this issue at the end of the book.

One last point on the concept of culture. Strategy and leadership create the crucible for success; they define how the organization is to be run. They decide on the best approaches to integrate all aspects and resources needed to grow and build their organization. The importance of this "cultural crucible" was demonstrated many years ago in activities related to performance improvement in other areas. Japan was seen (at the time) as the leader in "how to do things a different way" and many executives implemented Japanese approaches such as just in time delivery and manufacturing; lean concepts; statistical process control and many others.

They often failed because these approaches had been developed within a different culture. One of the most important books written about Japanese business practise was "Toyota Culture" written in 2008 which explained the "crucible" (my word) within which everything happened at Toyota.

Many executives and managers have brought in consultants, or tried themselves, to implement new systems and approaches to business only to see these efforts deliver less than anticipated results. The reason is almost always the lack of attention to the human aspect. Change involves people and the culture that they work in, will either help or hinder implementation of change.

Given that change is now, in many organizations, a permanent way of life, we can begin to see how important culture is, as a critical success factor. In summary, here is the journey we will describe, based on the PDCA approach:

PLAN	1. Make behaviour strategic
	2. Develop clear expectations
DO	3. Communicate and customize
	4. Hire the right talent
	5. Align HR framework
	6. Align policy and procedure
	7. Develop leadership
CHECK	8. Review everyone based on behaviour
ACT	9. Coach and support
	10. Continually improve

We use this model and explain each of the critical 10 steps to embed values based behaviours in everything an organization does. There are no short cuts or quick fixes. However, it will create a foundation for behavioural success - as important as Purpose.

Introduction summary
• Every organization has a culture; you actively manage it or "let it happen" with no guidance.
• Leadership statements, speeches and plaques are not enough.
• Values drive behaviour and behaviour drives "moments of truth" in every human interaction.
• Leadership at every level is responsible for ensuring behaviour ranks equally to "the task."
• Poor culture costs money - for many "you don't know what you don't know" and how this impacts cost and profitability.
• Behaviour must rank equally to mission, vision and purpose and be embedded with strategy, execution, measurement and improvements and changes.

Introduction checklist
• Does your organization have a "managed culture?"
• Do you believe that your culture is unique to your organization?
• Do common values drive behaviour and decision making?
• Is your culture part of long term strategy?

3 Strategy

This book will not rewrite everything that has been developed on strategy and planning but what it will do is show how existing systems can embrace on equal terms the actions necessary to elevate the human element. This will be done in a number of steps. First, we will place the human dimension within both a business model and a strategic framework to demonstrate how they can be integrated.

Next, we will move on to a "health check." This starts with a "where are you now" set of discovery options. It matters little where you think you are - in fact, this is often incorrect (or in some organizations delusional!). Following that, an organization, especially its leaders in terms of owners, board, and senior executives, needs to decide where they want to be in human strategy and the approach to behaviour. This will lead to both an exploration stage and the development of a set of behavioural principles around which everything else will be built. This stage will create a "gap analysis" and from this your first action plans will be developed.

All through his process, engagement of the people in the organization is critical. From clarification of the reality of the current situation, through development of a set of underlying principles, through to actual deployment and monitoring. This approach will fail if it is seen as something developed by management and handed down to everyone else. We will then move on to the steps needed to operationally embed these "intents" into the everyday reality of the business, including a broad based set of performance measures.

3.1 Framework for thinking and planning

Start by thinking about a high level business model that has been developed over the years to embrace the key aspects of operating a business. This is like context setting. We call this the 5P model.

Figure 2 The 5P Business Model

The model depicts the key building blocks for effective organizational management. The foundation is the organizational purpose - often incorporated in its vision and mission; however, added to "purpose" is beliefs and values. In effect purpose is to tasks and activities, what beliefs and values are to behaviour. This is the point of equal bias and is "P1"

Underlying EVERYTHING is the translation of the beliefs and values into an organizational culture (P2); this must permeate all actions that the organization takes to convert purpose into outcomes. It must create a "passion for the purpose" if it is to become "real" and become a strategic advantage. This creates the foundation for the next steps, in converting intent to execution which must be built on consideration of both what is to be done and how it is to be achieved.

The next level reflects the resources that are brought together to deliver on the plans. Processes (P3 - including machinery and equipment and all operational processes and tasks) focus on the operational "how" - the task. P4 reflects the human dimension to everything that needs to be done, using both internal and external resources - the "how" in terms of behaviour. Woven throughout both P3 and P4 will be the performance measures necessary to monitor achievement of the plans.

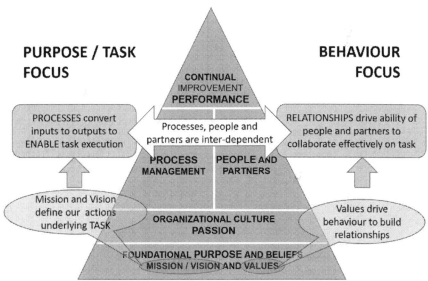

Figure 3 5P showing task and behaviour

Finally, P5 is effectively an outcome of the effective business model and that is a culture of continual improvement leading to "performance." The "5" in the model comes from the 5P's plus the conceptual goal of a five star (*****) performance rating.

One key business model for the ongoing operation of a business will be familiar to most managers. This is the PDCA or PDSA model; Plan, Do,

Check and Act. Historically this has been focused on the purpose and task aspect of business, but one can overlay the behaviour aspects using exactly the same approach:

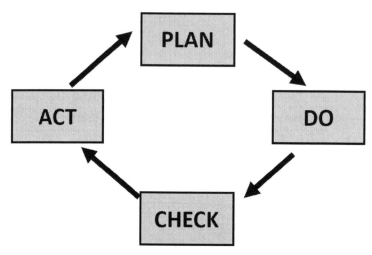

Figure 4 The basic PDCA model

Plans would incorporate both desired *operational outcomes* which typically drive organizational equipment and processes; the "tools" of the task. But equally plans must include the *desired behaviours*; for many organizations part of this may be already in place if behaviours drive some aspect of brand or reputation.

Next is the "do" aspect. This involves the "decomposition" of the desired operational outcomes into things like budgets, capital equipment purchases, supplier contracts. Again, it can equally include aspects of human resources management, especially leadership skills to translate the planned behaviours into action.

Thirdly we have the "Check." A large portion of checking is often around the ability to achieve task expectations (on time, quality, cost, quantity). However, again, there should be tools which provide feedback on how the expectations for behaviour are being operationally applied. Finally, the "Act" focuses on action necessary to keep "the plan on track" or to make corrective actions, or to incorporate changes into the next planning cycle. Behavioural aspects would equally fit in this category. Training, development, coaching, promotions, and other actions would be examples.

So, a new planning approach is not required. What is needed is an equal application of strategic "people behavioural planning" to an organization's strategies and plans, supported by an aligned follow through that aligns and supports every aspect of human interaction with the plans.

3.2 The big picture

Before any effort can be made to start embedding behavioural expectations into a business plan there needs to be a reality check. Every organization already has a culture and a way of operating; it has evolved over time. However, there are generally three situations.

A great organization (that might be able to ignore this whole book) has defined how it wants the organization to be seen in the way that it works. This organization's culture is "real," because it permeates everything that is done. Employees clearly understand how they are expected to interact with everybody else, and this can be relied upon; this includes every interaction, whether internally or externally. Everybody in a leadership position treats people fairly and reflects the corporate "way of doing things" on a consistent basis; trust is at a high level between and among people. Everyone's ideas are valued and respected; open communication, cooperation and collaboration are reflected in every human interaction. Outsiders see the organization as a "quality employer" and a valuable member of their community. When change it required, almost everybody approaches it with a positive an open attitude. There are lots more, but you get the idea.

On the other extreme is the organization where little attention is paid to behaviour on the assumption that people already know what is expected. It is assumed that they will act in the organizations best interest, but there are often situations where disciplinary actions have to be taken because employees take things into their own hands that cost the company money. There are sometimes surprises because people acted in a way that their manager or others did not expect. There seems to be some sort of feud or disagreement between departments.

Managers appear protective about their own organization and often seem less willing to collaborate and cooperate. Most people are only worried about their personal bonus - especially when it gets in the way of helping someone else. There may have even been serious problems when people thought they were doing the right thing to increase company revenues or profits - only to cause what others see as unethical actions. Change always seems a fight because there seems to be a lack of trust that management understands and appreciates the peoples own interests.

Finally, there is the middle of the road organization. There is a code of ethics in place and everyone has been exposed to it - maybe by the legal team did the training. The CEO and CFO are happy with signing off their statement of internal controls. Maybe the company has developed a set of "values" that it has posted everywhere in the company. There is a feeling, especially among senior managers that the "tone at the top" is good. That this is an ethical organization. Yet there still seem to be issues; regular fire-fighting of inter-departmental problems and lack of cooperation is an issue. Change is a challenge especially getting people "on board." It has been said that the organization "doesn't walk the talk."

In our first organization it would appear that has been and remains a focus on the culture. It has been planned and it appears to permeate every aspect of the business. One might compare this to one of Jim Collins "great" organizations (at least the ones' who have been able to sustain their position). It could also be like Johnson & Johnson whose corporate credo about how they operate was originally developed in 1943 and has guided the company since. These are not perfect organizations nor have they avoided problems, but they have had a "common guiding light" that has driven decision making.

The second group of organizations are those that usually focus most of their attention on financial performance and deal with the other aspects of business as "support activities." These organizations have increasingly run into behavioural problems as the human element has become more important. Examples would include banking and financial services; pharmaceutical companies; retailers; service organization; technology organizations, energy companies and others.

The last group of organizations probably represents the largest; they are committed to running an organization where behaviour matters yet there seem to be problems. All the right "speeches" from management have been made. Managers are always talking about how important the people are; there is even a framework of corporate values in place.

Many will remember Enron that had such as spectacular failure; here was a company that had a Code of Ethics that was over 60 pages, signed by the CEO. Surely behaviour was not going to be a problem. Another example, Carillion, a major UK construction company that collapsed in 2017 among scandals, had been given an award for its integrity and ethics.

As we move forward, we start with planning - following the mirror image of how we move forward on planning the overall business goals and objectives that align with the "purpose" - following the vision and mission. Many of these are inter-changeable terms so we have to be careful! In our discussion we will apply the following definitions:

- Purpose: "...the reason for which something exists or is done, made, used, etc. an intended or desired result; end; aim; goal."

- Values: "...guiding values are those characteristics that we commit to as individuals and as an organization so that we develop a culture that delivers our mission and executes our vision."

We will work on the basis that "Purpose" drives the planning for activities and tasks to achieve the "deliverable outcomes" of the business and to satisfy the reason "why" we are in business. "Values" are the underlying principles behind the "how" - of the behaviours that drive decision making as it relates to people and relationships.

One of the complexities of developing values as a foundation for human behaviour and relationships, is that behavioural activities (A) and outcomes (O) are both similar and iterative. For example, "you exhibit trust to create trust and become trustworthy." "You give respect to be respected" etc. etc. The challenge is to develop a few core values that can embrace and support the desired behaviours. The first set might be the "major 5:"

Behaviour	Comments	A	O
Collaborative	Co-labour - willingness to work jointly (with others) for the collective good.	X	X
Cooperative	Work jointly towards a common shared goal	X	X
Trust	Foster trust internally to become a trusted and trusting organization	X	X
Respect	Respect between people internally and externally fosters an organization that can be trusted	X	X
Integrity	"My word is my bond." Faithful: supports and complements commitment, integrity, and trust.	X	X

There are others that support, complement and add to the first 5. The right words are what "fit" the organization.

Behaviour	Comments	A	O
Ethical	Ethical behaviour creates a reputation for being ethical	X	X
Open	Being open denotes listening and sharing qualities, leading to a reputation of being open as an organization.	X	X
Learning	Fostering learning internally is a way to promote engagement and improvement.	X	
Committed	Commitment internally between and among people leads to an external willingness to commit to others such as clients.	X	X
Positive	Being positive is an attitude towards resolving differences and challenges.	X	X
Supportive	Being supportive internally fosters behaviours that create a reputation for being supportive to others externally.	X	X
Honest	Honesty is a foundation for communication and creates a climate for external honesty.	X	X
Inclusive	Inclusive denotes a willingness to engage equally with everyone. Embraces diversity.	X	X
Safe	Removes fear of retribution. Promotes honest interaction.	X	
Equality	Complements inclusive; engages all no matter their background or qualification.	X	X
Authentic	Complements honesty and promotes belief in relationships.	X	X
Recognition	Receiving feedback for contributions made no matter size or importance.	X	X

Having just "Purpose" and "Values" may not be the right words; some organizations use "Mission, Vision and Values," some have "Mission and

Corporate Philosophy." J&J call it their "Credo." They key is to have both Purpose and Behaviour included.

One word that might be seen as missing is "engaged;" this is an important behavioural aspect that is also an outcome. It is often used as a "collective umbrella" for all of the activities involved in an effective culture that result in "an engaged employee."

It reminds me of the story of the chicken and the pig, observing the farmer eating bacon and eggs for breakfast. The chicken pointed to the eggs proudly and said to the pig "See, I am engaged in the farmers breakfast." "Ah Yes," said the pig "but I am Committed." People can be engaged in the work of the business yet not be fully committed. Optimum potential is the goal.

For planning purposes, creating, and sustaining an effective culture is an enabling strategy for both enhanced performance and decreased risk. So, what are the business outcomes that an effective culture delivers because these will be the ultimate measures of success. What do successful and competitive organizations demonstrate?

- Innovative and creative.
- Customer or client focus.
- Social / societal awareness and responsibility.
- Attractive to others - (such as potential suppliers, clients, and employees).
- Trusted and ethical as seen by the community in general.
- Responsible and fair.
- Attractive investment - level of return and risk.

Creating all of these outcomes' rests heavily on the collective behaviours of the people involved in the conversion of inputs to outputs - the human aspect of the business model. In creating a series of values, leaders must be driven by understanding and promoting aspects of behaviour that create the climate with the highest potential of achieving and sustaining these outcomes.

Strategy summary
• Business models must provide equal value creation importance to task (purpose) and behaviour (values)
• Management systems, such as PDCA must reflect task and behaviour at every level equally.
• Behaviours must be based on a strategically developed definition of expectations aligned to outcomes.
• A set of principles that define expected values which drive behaviour are a core aspect of responsible governance.
Strategy checklist
• Are you committed to driving your future business equally on both task and behavioural outcomes?
• Is this equal commitment embedded as part of long term plans for the foundation of how you run the business?
• Do you know what your "current state" of culture and organizational behaviour is?
• Have you defined what values and behaviour should be based on your strategically important outcomes at the governance level?
• Do you know where you need to start (i.e., is there a gap and if so, how big?)
• Are the "words" being used relevant to the business and to the local society.
• Has there been broad engagement in understanding and developing the founding commitments and values?

4 Planning - Set the Foundations

Planning is "iterative" following the continuing PDCA cycle. What will be discussed in this chapter are actions required to create or validate the initial foundation for behaviours. Users can decide how best to apply the ideas. Planning means knowing where we are trying to go; here is a quick summary before we start the detailed planning.

First, we need to decide "where are we now?" Let us call it a health check. Even if there is an existing statement of values or code of conduct or ethics, we need to assess the degree to which it reflects what is desired and the level to which it is embedded. (If a statement of commitment is not in place, we need to create it). Second, we need to ensure that the behavioural values stated, reflect what the key stakeholders, especially the owners, want to commit to.

Third, we need to make sure that leadership is comfortable with what the values will mean in operational reality. We also need to ensure that what has been developed can be applied in the operational reality of the people who will be expected to reflect such behaviour.

Next, we need to embed the agreed values into the day-to-day reality of the business. This will be covered in Chapter 4. The first part of this is aligning the whole human resources management infrastructure, to underpin "system sustainability." We also need to make sure that the policies, procedures, and all approaches to work align with and support the intent of the values. Both these areas often cause a critical failure if not fully aligned.

Once the intended values have been "operationalized" it is critical that the metrics developed and used for managing organizational performance include both the task / process steps (purpose) and the values / behaviour steps. This will be the subject of Chapter 5.

Finally, we need to ensure that the information provided by both organizational learning, and performance measures results in change and improvement, either "real time" or as part of the planning cycle. These factors will be covered in Chapter 6.

4.1 Setting the direction

Before an organization can start planning to ensure it has an effective culture, there must be a reality check that asks, "where are we now?" This will take an organization beyond developing codes of conduct or statements of ethics. It will also need leaders to break an assumption that people know what is expected; (although people do learn what is expected, from those around them which they combine with their own personal belief systems and this is what creates an "unplanned" culture). There are several ways we can assess the current state.

4.1.1 Focus Groups

All focus groups should be broad based, confidential, and facilitated by an individual who is independent of both the people in the focus group and their management structure. This is to avoid bias wherever possible. Group sizes should be operationally and geographically diverse and limited in size to allow an adequate inter-change of views and ideas. If an organization operates in different geographic areas, where external cultures may vary, then views from these areas should also be sought and the data collected so as to be analyzed by area / region.

If there is an existing set of values, then a series of discussion questions can be prepared and used to evaluate the level of reality in place. To create the questions, the various items contained in the existing statement can be turned into questions. As an example, the statement "Employee ideas are important and valued" could be a discussed around "Are employee's ideas openly asked for" and "When you provide ideas, are they taken seriously?" The facilitator can then steer the conversation into understanding if there are "blockages" or fundamental differences between what is said and what is done (which will lead to actions to correct the situation).

If there is not an existing statement of values then the focus groups would be asked to identify what, based on the way in which the organization operates, they see as the underlying principles that drive company behaviour. A series of guiding discussion points could be created around key aspects of values related to trust, communications, cooperation, fairness, leadership consistency and possibly other areas of policy and procedure (some examples are in the appendix).

Focus groups can also be used externally; this is especially important where the organization has an existing brand, image, or reputation - part of which may be related to its interaction with customers in the marketplace. The same approach for focus groups, can be used based on the existence or absence of a statement of values. If there is not a clear statement, or if the people in the focus group do not seem aware of one, again it will be important to assess what reality they see being reflected by their dealings with the organization.

The same approach can be taken with other 3rd parties. For example, supply chain partnerships are critical to many organizations and the need to balance the drive for cost reduction with a strong relationship must be maintained. These focus groups would identify the reality at the working level between buyers and sellers. If there is a high level of interaction with regulators or others, then again, this same approach could be taken.

The result from these focus groups will provide a strong reality check on what these people see as the principles that drive the relationships both inside and outside the organization. It will also provide a sound foundation for continual improvement and "gap closing strategies" for driving operational changes.

4.1.2   Surveys

Surveys are often fraught with dangers. The surveys often fail to ask the right questions and when the results have been tabulated, employees often observe that nothing changes. Recognizing this, the best surveys are developed by a working group representing a cross section of the people to be covered by the surveys. They will develop the questions. They will also form a "sounding board" on the responses, to help interpret what the results seem to reflect.

Survey questions can again be developed around an existing statement of values or conduct, or they can start with a generic set of questions built around typical underlying indicators of an effective culture; examples are given in the appendix.

4.1.3   Informal assessment

There will be organizations that want to take a "low key" approach to understanding their current culture or validating their state of health. In this case independent third parties, such as consultants can be brought in to spend some time visiting company locations and talking to staff individually. It will be important that these people have "independence to roam" or once again their input may be biased. The danger of this approach is that it might be seen as a management initiative and either the feedback to management might be felt to be biased or the individual(s) may be personally biased, or people will tell the third party "what they think they want to hear."

The best solution might be to combine focus groups with the independent third party to enhance the belief in the objectivity of the exercise.

4.1.4 Where do you want to go?

While the above steps are designed to assess "what is" a similar data gathering step must be developed at the owner and leadership level. This will either affirm what has already been stated, or it will provide the foundation for the values and reputation the owners want the organization to embody. It is important at this level of discussion to consider the relationship between society values and the way the organization operates.

It is common knowledge that the values of society have been changing quite rapidly over recent decades and organizations who fail to adapt to recognize and reflect these changes operate at a higher risk. This risk extends to both lenders' recognition of the greater risks but also issues like "attractiveness" to key human talent and customer perceptions. An example would be a commitment to operating on a "sustainable" basis from an environmental perspective. There will be positives from an organization reflecting a commitment to goals like "zero carbon" and also negative impacts from not doing so. There are also risks associated with "saying the words" but not delivering - called "greenwashing" if it reflects environmental commitments.

It is also that those establishing the values consider the history and tradition of the organization. Are there things that the organization built its' reputation on that must be perpetuated?" Are there areas of zero tolerance where, if there is to be a trade off, one thing is more important than the other? Are there areas which the organization must avoid "at all costs" that would clearly be seen as detrimental to its brand and reputation? Establishing organizational values as a foundation for behaviour is as strategically critical as establishing corporate purpose. Both will set the foundation for decision making including the allocation of resources.

There are some foundational aspects of behavioural values that must be included. There must be a commitment to both legal and ethical behaviour; in todays environment where decision making has been pushed lower and many more people are now decision makers, it is a requirement that every single person commits to this principle. It is also critical because a large portion of internal control rests with individual decisions made at every level.

4.1.5   Building the base

Using the combination of either an existing statement of values or the intended direction set by the owners or board the process of developing a foundational set of corporate values can start. If the foundation is a new set, then the comparison of "new to existing" will form the basis of moving forward. If there is an existing set, then the discussion will be about affirming or modifying the stated values and assessing the actions needed to close gaps that appear to exist between the owner's intent and reality.

Either way, a foundational set of organizational values can be created that will form the basis of behaviour among and between people both inside and outside the organization.

4.2   Are you sure you know what this means?

One of the biggest problems in organizational behaviour is the gap that appears between base line stated values and operational reality. A critical first step, before any level of deployment, is for the owners and leaders to evaluate whether there is a shared and committed understanding of what the words used in the values will actually mean.

Typical values statements are composed of short statements about specific commitments but, being short, they are often open to wide interpretation, as they are deployed down through the organization. They can also be misinterpreted at the executive leadership level, that results in an inconsistent approach to management across the business. This is why there is an "Is / Is Not" step at this point; this goes beyond the simplicity of the statement and asks, "what might this mean operationally?"

The process starts by taking each individual statement at its face value and then stimulating a discussion about what this might mean when it is read and translated operationally; this process is critical at the executive level but should also be done as the values are cascaded down the organization. This is the only way to convert a high level statement of intent into a "what does this mean to me in my job" statement. The approach is quite simple, and the outcome can be shown on a document such as the following:

To be recognized as a leader in our relationships with employees	
(Is) This means	**Is not (Do not do this)**
❑ Fostering trust, communication, and inclusiveness. ❑ Provide equal opportunity. ❑ To listen and to show concern / empathy. ❑ Show care, respect, and acknowledgement of all. ❑ Provide a safe workplace - physically, emotionally & mentally. ❑ Set clear guidelines for expected performance and behaviour. ❑ Be consistent in our approach to discipline and rewarding performance. ❑ Maintain a high level of employee satisfaction and low turnover.	❑ Inconsistency in dealing with employees in different departments or locations. ❑ Abiding by minimum standards vs. leading practice. ❑ Accepting the minimum required performance of employees. ❑ Deviating from our stated Values in dealing with employees ❑ Allowing employees to engage in activities "disrespectful" of our Values.

Figure 5 Example of "Is / Is Not" worksheet

In this example the stated value is at the top of the sheet, and then the results of the discussion about what this means operationally is below

- showing what we would be doing and what we would NOT be doing. The result of this exercise might be either a clarification or a change of the stated value to ensure that the commitment can be followed through with actions that support and affirm the stated value.

This process is critically important the larger the organization becomes, especially when different geographies contribute to different local cultures. In many large organizations the high level statements of values are often reworked and reworded, so as to remain consistent with "the parent" but be more relevant and applicable to the local business unit. The "Is / Is Not" step is also critical because different levels and locations will have different interpretations.

Leaders need to be clear of the intent because decision making flows from values commitments. As an example, an organization that commits to go "above and beyond" minimum employment standards, including areas such as health and safety will require a financial commitment to make that a reality. Not doing so, in order to meet financial goals would render the values statement untrue and present employees with a different reality.

By this stage, the organization has established a foundation for the behaviours that it expects to take place. These will have been embedded in the planning stage of the PDCA in a way that focuses both on (traditional) purpose - the "what" of the organization's existence PLUS on ensuring that the desired behaviours leading to an effective culture have been developed. Planning must reflect changes in the marketplace, the capabilities of the organization *and the needs of society within which it operates.*

Values are now given an equal weighting to Purpose, to identify how the organization wants to (establish and) perpetuate "the way we do things around here." This complements the purpose but deals with the behaviours. (There may be aspects of this that have traditionally been addressed within "Purpose." As an example, if the environmental scan or a

PEST or PESTLE evaluation looked at the social and societal impacts that surround the "purpose" but with a human-centric organization, the planning approach to setting goals and objectives for behaviour must get equal attention). The "Plan" step is now integrated and completed - People Plus Purpose.

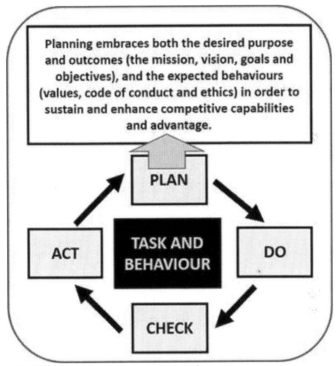

Figure 6 PDCA Step 1 Planning - Purpose + Values

The plans now need to be deployed. Setting in place the "Do's" for planning is about making things happen. Decomposing the intent in the plans, to specific tactics and actions through which intent is converted to reality. Equal attention must be given to both the processes, plans and actions and to the leadership of the people who are to undertake this.

The "P" - Planning summary
• The planning stage of PDCA must include a detailed assessment of both "what is" and where you are now.
• Employees and others (e.g., external) must be included as part of this approach.
• Thought must be given to the linkage between "brand value" and the behavioural drivers of brand and reputation.
• The formulation of values MUST include clarification of operational understanding through as "Is / Is Not" discussion.
• Part of the "Current State" might already be part of a PEST or PESTLE approach to planning.
The "P" - Planning checklist
• Have the underlying values been broadly discussed?
• Have all levels of employees been involved?
• Have non-employees been involved (supplier, customer, distributor, subcontractor etc.)
• Has the list been reduced to the critical few that are strategic to organisational sustainability?
• Has management remained open to the reality as seen by other stakeholders?
• Have "zero tolerance" aspects been included to ensure adequate attention?
• Has planning been "cascaded" both across and down the organization to ensure the right fit?
• Is the outcome of this step adequate for those required to develop deployment / execution tactics?
• Has "space" been left for iteration between specified expectations and adjustments for deployment reality?

5 Do - Operational alignment

The first and most critical "line of defence" is the alignment between organizational values and leadership behaviour. Starting at the board or owner level there must be a commitment to act in accordance with the values. Because each person is a unique human being, having their own personality, values, and beliefs, this can be a key challenge. The underlying human resources management system that we will discuss, is established to underpin, and support the defined values. However, in creating the foundation both during initial "roll out" or in a refreshment approach, validating this commitment must take place. There is no point in going any further or making any commitments, if the people in leadership positions at any level in the organization, do not personally commit to accepting and supporting the values.

There is a process to do this that can be thought of as a personal "gap closer." It also might lead to further discussions on the organizational commitment to certain values and to personal development plans for existing people in leadership positions. An example of the "tool" is in the appendix; for each value which is stated a series of questions are asked and five levels of possible response are given. The questions are:

- I understand what this value means.
- As a manager, I choose this value freely.
- I publicly affirm this value.
- I prize and cherish this value.
- I act on this value consistently.

For each question, a rating is given from 1 (Strongly disagree) to 5 (Strongly agree) together with a comments section. While there is no "pass or fail" this process allows an assessment of leadership support for each value. If there is a trend of low scoring among leaders this might indicate a problem with the stated value which might need further discussion.

It could also mean that there is a strong need for development of managers. It might also identify some specific issues and problems where managers are "not a good fit", in terms of their leadership skills. This is not unusual; the transition to a human centric organization has shifted core manager skills much higher in the leadership area. Some may have been appointed managers with great technical skills but are not able to exercise the leadership skills required.

Selecting managers for the future will include assessments of their personal alignment with organizational values. This process will be covered next in getting the human resources infrastructure strategically aligned.

5.1 Strategically driven, integrated HR management
The whole framework for human resources management must be driven by, and aligned with, the strategic importance of people to the organization. Focusing on assessing and hiring people with the "right attitude" has become equally important to seeking the required skills and capabilities. There is a whole life cycle framework that impacts people management, and this must ensure that "the right people are on the bus." It must also ensure that the environment for people in terms of HR plans, policies, and procedures all reflect and support the stated values of the organization.

There are a few core processes that HR designs and manages, that are critical for values alignment. These are:
- Hiring - planning and selection of people.
- Orientation / on-boarding.

- Development - reviews, succession plans and actions.
- Promotion - especially into leadership roles.
- Disputes - complaints, and whistle-blowing.

These activities, involving getting the right people in the right place must give equal importance to the skills and capabilities and to personality and behaviour.

Hiring is making an investment. The process requires resources and demonstrates to prospective candidates the type of behaviour the organization supports. Many organizations have already changed and improved their approach to hiring; however, both the interview process and the final selection must include an assessment of the individuals "fit" with the stated values of the organization. You can fill gaps in skill sets by development and training, but it is hard to correct deeper attitude concerns.

Tools are available to help assess underlying personalities and attitudes; additional tests such as case studies and vignettes can be developed for discussion with the candidate to assess how they might act in certain situations where behaviour is important. The company values could also be discussed specifically to ensure acceptance and "fit." Peer interviews can also be helpful. Psychometrics can play a role here and these are briefly referred to in Chapter 7.

Once the candidates have been hired, initial exposure to and development in the organizational values must occur. This must be seen as equally important as not allowing a factory employee on the production floor without safety training. Orientation cannot be deferred and must take place before the new employee interacts with others in or outside the organization.

Once people are on board, the next group of activities relate to their ongoing development - progress reviews, training, consideration for transfers or promotions. The approach needs to again align with values; supportive of people - not judgemental; seeking to coach and support; focusing on strengths but trying to build on these while trying to minimize areas of less strength and complement these with the skills of others. In particular, reviews should be focusing on collaborative, cooperation, and communication skills with others. Any sort of evaluation must include assessment of the ability to embrace and demonstrate the behavioural qualities that support the organizations values.

One key challenge in "living the values" is the need for results on the purpose / task side; there must be adequate recognition that achieving task is important but in doing so the values must be respected. Relationships must not be set as a lower priority than results, as an effective relationship takes time to build and is a valuable "asset" to the business. Not paying attention to this aspect may mean achievement of short term results but the trade-off might be the impairment or destruction of important relationships.

For the development of managers and others in a leadership role (such as team leaders), any feedback or review must include input from metrics designed to evaluate "demonstration of the values." For a culture to take root and prosper, people in leadership positions are "the gardeners," They are required to take the time and effort to ensure that in good times and bad, values drive behaviour. It is often said of managers "it is not the 95% you do right but the 5% you do wrong" that people remember. It is also critical that people in leadership positions in a hierarchy are seen as being supported by those above them.

Many mid level managers are often placed in an impossible situation, where they are unable to uphold values because of poor communications with those above. This would also apply to managers having flexibility to manage their own group of people. It is they, who have the closest relationships where trust is being built. This is why the "buy in" to values starts at the top and cascades down. If there is not consistency and reasonable level of harmony, trust, collaboration, and cooperation at the senior level it is unlikely to be seen at lower levels.

Succession planning is an important part of perpetuating the values; promotions from within allow "learnings" about the inner workings of the organization and its culture to be retained and further embedded. This is not to say "new blood" may not be required, but an organization that takes the long view and takes the time to develop its own succession chain will have a greater chance of perpetuating the desired organizational culture. As a slight digression, this is often a problem when a merger or acquisition occurs; different cultures try and come together and often neither works effectively; this results in a failure to meet anticipated benefits from the combination. The "crucible" that had been created in each organization that underpinned its "way of doing things" is upended.

Talent management, as an aspect of succession planning is also critical. The people with the greatest potential and the greatest value to the organization generally want a challenge. If promotion comes "too slowly" they might be lost to a competitor. This is not just a demographic issue; organizations need to provide the challenges that potential future leaders need, so as to keep them around. HR approaches must be creative using ideas such as secondments to suppliers, projects with clients and customers, executive interchanges with maybe government, internal projects, secondments to other divisions and locations, international postings, and many others. But again, these must clearly support the values of the organization. Some people may have limitations for family reasons or other personal challenges. The organization needs to work with this reality.

Another key demonstration of values comes with organizational change where people in certain locations might face job loss, or technologies change, leaving some people unable to adapt. How the organization handles these situations, will demonstrate a great deal about values. If people are valued, then the organization will plan for these changes with the impact of people high on its agenda. Across the board layoffs (in any situation) give a clear (poor) message about the value of people. However, if the organization assigns resources to help and support these people, that will also send a clear (better) message. The memory that must be left behind is that "the organization did their best to help me." There are no "jobs for life" but there are organizations who honour their commitments to people.

Dealing with "problems and disputes" is another key area where values must be clearly woven through an organizations HR processes. The approach must be open and fair. In cases where performance expectations are not being met there must be adequate investigation into underlying reasons. Personality conflicts and labelling people as "lazy" should be avoided. Where there are issues, they must be clearly communicated and documented. They must be fact based with the facts being openly shared.

If need be, a third party must be involved in problem resolution especially where a relationship has become adversarial. Alternative solutions must be offered and if all else fails, a fair resolution must result if there is not a good fit. In dealing with people, the HR approaches must be capable of dealing with the "whole person" not just during the hours they are at the organization. This will require having confidential, external advisory or support services available for individuals to access.

Dealing with serious issues such as contravention of legal or ethical requirements must be taken seriously with an impartial observer involved. All cases must be thoroughly investigated. This can be a problem where an organization chooses to have employees escalate problem ethical issues for resolution by others at more senior levels. They might feel the problem has been "swept under the carpet." Often when problem issues arise, they are handled by the legal department which is a major challenge. Because something is not illegal does NOT mean it might be unethical or in contravention of an organizations stated "values." This can be an important source of an organization being perceived as "not living the values."

There are many other areas of HR activity not discussed here in detail however every single policy, procedure and process that causes an interaction with an employee is a "moment of truth." Pay must be seen to be fair and equitable; benefits must be seen to exceed the minimum necessary. Unfair practices relative to the employment of part time or temporary staff must be avoided as again they deliver a message of values. Compensation for employee expenses must be fair and reasonable both in amounts and speed of reimbursement. Working conditions, whether in a factory, restaurant, office or other must be consistent with values. There was a consultant several years ago that believed you could assess management's commitment to its employees by looking at the washrooms!

5.2   Alignment of policy and procedures

One of the greatest problems is building an effective culture is the existence of policies and procedures that either do not align with or clearly conflict with stated values. There may be various reasons for this; first "functional silos" tend to develop policies and procedures that do not consider the impact of their application on people's attitudes and motivations. Another issue is that in many cases the impact of levels of employee motivation cannot be easily measured and so compliance with policies and procedures takes place but reduces an employee's motivation because, to them "it doesn't make sense."

I always wished I had reacted to an example I overhead at a meeting of senior executives. One VP was complaining to the CEO about an accounting policy that forced them to take a flight rather than the train. This was in Europe where high-speed train travel is widely available and although it may take longer, if one considers the wait times involved with airline travel the "total trip time" is not that much different. The air fare was lower, but the VP complained that while they could do a lot of work in comfort on the train, trying to do this on an aircraft would be more difficult. The extra expense cost would be MORE than offset by gaining valuable hours of executive "knowledge application" time. The CEO was obliged to ensure that VP's followed procedures and that was the result. This just does not make logical sense, but financially - where it shows up and can be measured it looks like a cost saving. The "apparent savings" was a few hundred Euros. If the executive salary were even €150,000 annually, a few hours added time would at least equal the travel cost saving - yet the policy did not encourage a productive use of time, appearing to be focused on saving money. This is where conflict occur and there are plenty of examples.

Figure 7 Example of policy & procedure validation

EduVision Inc.	Policy and Values Validation					
Client						
Policy / Procedure	Value #1	Value #2	Value #3	Value #4	Value #5	Value #6
HR Policies (e.g.)						
Hiring policy and procedure						
Promotion policy and procedure						
Wage and salary policies						
Sickness / time off						
Vacation and time off policy and procedure						
Discipline procedure						
Education and tuition policy & procedure						
Accounting Policies (e.g.)						
Travel policy						
Expense reimbursement						

One important way to resolve this is to implement an approach such as this. In this checklist each policy and procedure are compared to each of the corporate values and scored on its level of consistency. Yes, this can be a long exercise, but it is the only way that alignment between task and behaviour can be achieved. The scoring system is looking for the "level of fit and reinforcement" that aligns "what you say and what you do." The scoring system might look something like this:

Score	Weight	Criteria
+3	Positive	There is a highly positive correlation and alignment between the organizations policy / procedure and the organizations stated values. Practicing this policy or procedure will reinforce the stated values and contribute toward credibility in our values.
+2		There is reinforcement of the organizations values and the policy / procedure is aligned but more could be done to improve the relationship
+1		There is a slight positive aspect to the policy or procedure relative to the organizations values but it does not strongly reinforce them
0	Neutral	Policy or procedure neither supports or reinforces the organizations values statements
-1	Negative	There is a slightly negative relationship between this policy / procedure and the organizations stated values; it will not have significant impact but should be corrected
-2		There is a disconnect between this policy / procedure and the organizations stated values and this should be corrected
-3		There is a strong and clear inconsistency between this stated policy / procedure and the stated values of the organization. Continuing to follow this approach will create inconsistency, negatively impact morale and demonstrate a lack of credibility between what we say and what we do.

Figure 8 Policy / Procedure and Values Scoring

Starting at the top, a highly correlated and mutually supportive connection between stated values and the policy and procedure would score a "3." Both the +3 and +2 could be marked "green" as good correlation. Then +1, 0 and -1 would be marked amber as a warning of a higher risk between what you say and what you do. Finally, -2 and -3 would be marked red and would clearly indicate significant risk because to follow the stated policy or procedure would conflict with what has been stated as its values.

41

This process of alignment needs to follow through every aspect to ensure that both internally and externally there is a consistent approach. This includes:

- Supplier relationships (at all levels e.g., design, development, purchasing, operations, accounting).
- Customers and clients - again at all levels, sales, shipping, billing, credit, returns, service.

In order to address the "moments of truth" organizations should think about EVERY interaction both internally and externally and provide guidance. First, the question of values in terms of "what does this mean to me in my job?" will be answered. Second wherever possible, people will look to the values to guide their behaviour.

However, there is one BIG problem here and that is the number of interactions that are NOT covered by policies or procedures. Situations that "fall between the cracks" and result in the individual employee having to decide. This is where the "indoctrination" of the values in natural behaviours wherever possible becomes important. The employee should know that "when in doubt do the right thing based on our stated values."

This might worry many managers. It leaves them open to being responsible for the independent behaviour of their staff. In todays competitive environment, stopping to escalate problems and issues can encourage bureaucracy. This is NOT the answer. If this is used, it also tends to reduce trust. Employees, if hired with the right attitude, led with a supportive manager, and allowed to make their own decisions, trust will build.

There is a risk here. Sometimes an employee maybe makes what they think is the right decision, but it turns out to either cost money or not be the best alternative. This is NOT a discipline problem - but a learning opportunity. The best story I ever heard about this, even if it sounds unbelievable) came from the airline industry.

I was working at Vancouver (Canada) airport leading a consulting project and was told about a pushback tractor operator who had misjudged his clearance when he was backing an aircraft out of the hangar. The result was a scrape on the fuselage that grounded the aircraft (an expensive mistake). Watching the incident was the VP of Engineering whose office overlooked the hangar floor. He came down after seeing the incident and many employees expected to see the operator being fired on the spot. However, after inspecting the damage the VP asked the operator why it had happened and at the end of the explanation, he said he was sorry and was expecting to be fired. "Fired," questioned the VP? "I am not firing you. I just invested thousands of dollars in an expensive training episode. Will you ever make that mistake again?"

The damage was done, and nothing was going to undo it. The best that could happen is that it was avoided in the future. The motivational impact would have been incredibly high and there was no need for a shouting episode - I am sure that the employee already felt bad enough.

Organizational values provide a rich training ground for managing in the spaces caused by events, that cannot be pre-determined. If it turns out, because of inexperience an employee makes the wrong decision, then as long as it was driven by a clear logical link to the values then it should be supported. If there was an alternative action that could have been taken this is a learning opportunity.

5.3   Managing in the spaces

No amount of policy and procedure can cover every eventuality; additionally, too much policy and procedure create added cost to maintain, and bureaucracy to implement. Todays organizations, seeking to be lean, responsive, and competitive, as well as "great to do business with" want to remove as many barriers as possible. This requires building a level of consistency and predictability on human actions. Part of the underlying issue with scandals such as Wells Fargo is probably that well intentioned people did the wrong things for what they thought were the right reasons. Often conflicting message between incentive pay and organizational values reinforce this problem. This unpredictability creates a significant risk for organizations and is one key reason why values have become so important.

5.3.1 Internal control: The Cultural Gorilla

As people and their behaviour have become more important, organizations have struggled by the whole issue of controls. Yet, in spite of new legislation such as SOX and additional oversight for public company's and the audits such as PCAOB and the FCA there seem to have been increasing level of "behavioural problems." Much of this lies at heart of the transformation necessary to embed an effective culture. As stated earlier, creating a code of ethics or a code of conduct statement - or even a statement of corporate values, and putting them on the wall. Is nowhere near an effective solution. It is like "rearranging the deck chairs on the Titanic."

Behavioral predictability is always going to be a challenge because people are, by definition prone to independent action. As organizations strive to greater flexibility and innovation, those concerned with internal controls, especially accounting and legal, struggle to manage risk. This has been made worse because advances that have been made in psychology have, on the one hand, provided great tools in understanding personality and different tendencies to act in certain ways but, on the other hand they have also taught us that people are strongly driven by emotions and can be unpredictable. Even the study of economics, that for many years was based on a model that assumed the rational response of people to things like prices and availability, has been changed because the assumptions of rationality are no longer a predictable result.

The reliance on predictable human behaviour has again been made more complex because mobility on both a national and global level has inter-mingled people with different backgrounds and personal values in a common environment. The results will be unpredictable if not managed. People are generally not good or bad, but they are different; a major reason is that they have different backgrounds that create both different values and different attitudes.

For many organizations this again increases risk because the "expected" behaviour may not be "natural" to certain individuals. The challenge for a business is managing this risk. The goal needs to be "just in control." Too many controls will stifle innovation, creativity, and self motivation. Too little control and there is no predictability. There is a natural tension here - people in charge of risk management want it minimized so seek more control; entrepreneurs and leaders want the approach to allow some level of risk.

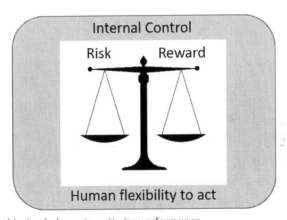

Figure 9 Achieving balance to optimize performance

This challenge is a particular problem in ethics - especially in an economic system driven by the profit motive. Whether expectations are defined by law or "expected" because of ethics, these may not be the traditional way that an employee thinks, works, and makes decisions. So, an effective culture is a mandatory aspect of internal control. Just checking on the tone at the top is not enough to verify predictability of compliance.

As stated, this becomes riskier as decisions and actions are not covered by policies and procedures. Human behaviour must be part of both risk assessment and systems of internal control. Having a well defined and implemented culture will be a core part of this control.

5.3.2   Allowing Leaders to Lead

Another critical area of values deployment is at the workgroup level; this is where the closest relationships are developed and where the reality of values and personality are most often demonstrated. Two things (at least) are critical at this level for the leaders of the workgroup. First, they must fundamentally believe in the values of the organization because the day-to-day decisions they make in managing activity will deliver moments of truth. This is why the initial buy-in, as well as the importance of hiring, orientation and promotion for leadership roles must be diligent.

Secondly, the workgroup leaders will tend to develop an understanding of their unique group of people. It is at this level that the creation of a motivating environment tales place. This is the unique "crucible" for the people in the workgroup. While it needs to demonstrate consistency and commonality when dealing outside the group, the longest and deepest relationships will be within the group.

The leader must therefore have some level of flexibility to encourage, reward and develop people within their group in a way that they see as most relevant. It may seem a small issue, but constraints such as not allowing the manager to treat everyone to a pizza dinner, after a project is completed, can be both demoralizing and demotivating for staff as well as for the manager. Approaches to both financial budgeting as well as delegations of authority can either be a supporting factor to values or a damaging one.

A final world on leaders and workgroups. The comments made above relate at all levels and the sad factor is that in many organizations, the more senior the manager the greater flexibility. If there is not some level of consistency all the way through, this can again raise questions about "living the values." What people see is what they believe. Inequity between areas and people can be quite damaging; while it is often a reality, it must be seen as fair and reasonable. This can include the obvious issues like pay and benefits but also extend to issues like computer hardware and parking spaces. Remember that people are not always rational and are driven by emotional reaction.

5.3.3   Social Change: The Other Elephant in the Room

Organizational values must, to a reasonable extent, align with and reflect societal values. This requires that development and deployment of values, at all the stages discussed, needs to be implemented within a structure that recognizes different societal values. As an example, if a US based company develops a set of values, while these must be the foundation of the global organization, implementation must be done on a geographic basis recognizing the uniqueness of each group and culture. A sure way to increase the risk of deployment is to try and force everyone to comply with a single interpretation of the values.

This is a core area where mergers and acquisitions fail; not only are there problems between different organizational cultures, but there are also often major differences because of geographic reasons. An example of this, although there are many, is the case study of the merger between US based Chrysler and German based Daimler-Benz. On paper, they were complementary. At the person to person collaboration, communication, and cooperation level they were not, and it failed (with a massive loss to shareholders).

This is another area where leadership is important; if management "from the top down" is not agreed on values and seems reluctant to adapt and evolve, rather trying to create a "force fit," then that resistance will be seen throughout the organization. Where this REALLY becomes a problem, is when the foundations of societal values are changing. An example is the focus on equality and diversity. While having these expectations written into legislation is good, that will not make change happen. No amount of policy or quota or reporting will drive the change. It will only happen at the personal level on a one-on-one basis. If an organization has, embedded in its values the beliefs in equality and diversity than this will only become real when it becomes "the way we do things around here." Once again it requires "attitude change." This must start with a buy-in by anyone in a manager or leader position. If mandatory diversity training is implemented and managers reluctantly give up their staff to attend, but do not demonstrate belief in the concept, it will be a complete waste of time and money. To send people on this important type of development and change activity with a "nod, nod, wink, wink - I know its not important but we have to do it" attitude, will not only confuse employees, but it will also guarantee failure.

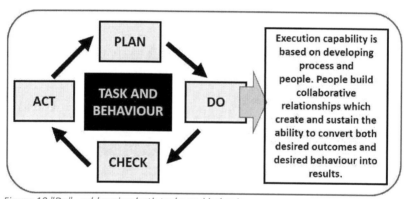

Figure 10 "Do" - addressing both tasks and behaviours

The PDCA approach has now dealt with the "Do" aspects relative to both tactics for the process side of converting inputs to outputs as well as the HR systems and supports and the behavioural expectations while the work is being executed. There are no "values short cuts." No consultants can come in and make it happen. No program of workshops on values, will may them believable. Day-by-day, moment of truth by moment of truth, is the only way. Not a program. Just the way we do things round here.

The "D" - Doing. Operational summary
• All aspects of the HR framework must align with and underpin the desired values and behaviours.
• Employee selection is a critical success factor in enabling the desired culture. (Psychometrics can provide support).
• Orientation / On-boarding are as critical for enabling culture as safety training is for health and safety.
• Focused attention to those placed in ANY leadership position is critical for sustaining culture.
• All leaders must embrace the values and demonstrate them through their leadership behaviour on ALL occasions.
• All Operational Policies, Procedures, Instructions, and all supporting materials must reflect and support the desired behaviours.
• All existing "process" materials must be evaluated, scored, and aligned to reflect the desired behavioural expectations.
• Internal controls and risk management must be directly integrated with behavioural expectations.
• Behavioural alignment must extend to external relationships such as suppliers and customers.
• Deployment will be an on-going challenge, but the commitment must be embedded and constant.
• There must be a log term commitment to training, coaching, and supporting at both the individual and work group level to perpetuate the desired behaviours.
• Any mergers, acquisitions of other "group integrations" will require a specific plan and assessment for cultural impact.

The "D" - Doing. Operational checklist
• Has every aspect of HR management been reviewed for strategic alignment? Including selection and hiring, promotions, orientation, pay and benefits, evaluations, coaching, development, counselling etc.
• Has every person in a leadership position (as a minimum) "bought in to" the desired values?
• If there are challenges with people in leadership roles, do their development plans include addressing and resolving these problems?
• Are plans in place to ensure "the right people are on the bus?"
• Are all operating procedures aligned with values? E.g., Travel and time off policies, overtime, operational (e.g., quality, service, client support, returns, credit), financial / accounting (e.g., credit and collections, payroll processes, expense reimbursement, allowances for tools and equipment etc.)
• Has the "Is / Is Not" discussion taken place as the expected behaviours are cascaded through the organization?
• Have those been involved with supply chain integrity been fully engaged in sharing / using behaviours with suppliers?
• Are sales policies, incentives and approaches consistent with desired behaviours?
• Are contractual and legal approaches consistent with desired values and behaviours?
• Are there ongoing reinforcement activities in place with "team coaches" for problem solving and sustaining values?
• Have steps been taken to ensure "cultural sustainability" when key leaders change position, retire, or leave?

6 Check - Measurement alignment

The "Check" aspect of embedding "values" into an organization serves two purposes. First it will tell how well the planned implementation of values is driving the reality of behaviours in and around the organization. "Are the moments of truth" delivering a consistent message? But it is also strategic in that it starts to develop metrics that can be utilized in both internal and external reporting of "human capital."

Although many organizations have identified the need for such metrics including the SEC as of November 2020, the need has been poorly satisfied. This is a major problem. For organizations, the amount of investment in people is probably one of the greatest expenses and has become one a significant driver of value creation. Yet there is little understanding of either the people risk, the "culture" of the organization or the level of financial investment. Developing this part of PDCA offers a great opportunity.

The book is about corporate culture, so by design we will not stray into tracking and reporting of financial aspects, although there are financial aspects of creating and sustaining an effective culture that should be part of accountability. What is the goal of measuring culture? Outcomes are critical - is the culture that we have fostering the behaviour that is needed to deliver the desired performance? Activity measures will also be important as they track whether the ongoing day-by-day activities are "in control" and progressing in a manner that supports the outcomes desired. This is where we will focus. In order to identify what needs to be measured we need to reflect on why we would want to focus on culture. The answer was that *it fosters an environment where people can work at their optimum level of performance* - culture Is an "enabler." Let us look at how the issue of culture fits into optimizing people in the organization.

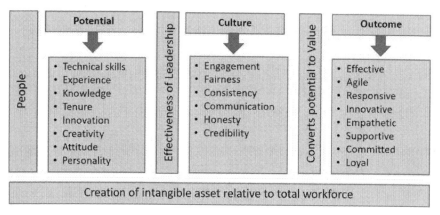

Figure 11 Culture as people enabler

Although people are not an asset in the traditional sense, they have been selected by the organization for a specific purpose - usually driven by skills, capabilities, qualifications, experience and hopefully, attitudes. Like a factory without the power turned on, they have potential.

But potential is not what creates value; it contributes to it, but it is energized by the "crucible" that we talked of earlier. The core role of leadership (from the highest level) is to create the most positive environment possible within which the talent that is available, can contribute their best. This is where culture fits - it is the energizer between potential and performance. An organization can have the most experienced and talented people but can fail to excel through poor leadership. So, the measurements needed should demonstrate that the required environment is being sustained and the desired outcomes are being achieved.

I remember a quote that supports what effective organizations achieve. "Great things can be done by motivated groups of average people." In an organization, there is always the need for specialist and individuals with unique talents, but it is a rare organization that does not require some level of collective effort to achieve it goals and objectives. Many have responded to this reality by teambuilding and other models. These will help but I would suggest that you don't "fire the coach once training is over?" Team development is NOT an event but an ongoing coaching activity (in fact if it is done as an event it will probably deplete the culture."

Figure 12 Continual team development framework

This is why in our book on "Reflective Leaders" we suggested an alternative approach to team development. (This is raised because it has implications for measurement). There are similarities and consistencies between the team development steps and the PDCA stages of an overall business model. "Formation" is the stage where potential is brought together; deliberation is about the planning for "how do we want to be." For a team or workgroup this would include the adoption of the values within which the group works.

It can be seen that this development model specifically supports and aligns with the steps that are being discussed applying the PDCA approach. The important issue is that there is no end point. This fully supports and reflects the importance of culture. It is not a program; not a one shot deal but a continual way of operating.

Figure 13 Core steps in embedding values and culture

When approaching measurement, aim for simplicity - a few measures linked to critical strategy. Avoid using measures as a way to either single out individuals or "sit in judgement." The behaviours desired, are there to optimize process performance, so these are the drivers of effectively performing task and activities.

Creating the culture is a journey so measures need to assess" how progress is being made in creating and sustaining the desired work environment" and "how well are the outcomes being achieved." One could minimize outcome measures, because employee retention, profitability and happy customers are the main goals. Success can be measured in organizational "system" term such as:

- Quality - meets requirements, right first time every time in product, service, and relationship.
- Output/productivity - continually enhanced effectiveness; being able to do "more for less"
- Revenue - growth in terms of total system output (including impact of innovation).
- Cost - lower cost / unit of output through enhanced innovation for both design and process.

The measures are going to be both objective and subjective and should be reviewed and primarily used as indicators of trends. There should be measures for activities and outcomes and a monitoring of opinions. Organizations should avoid heavy reliance on employee surveys as, traditionally administered these are often too slow and lack credibility.

However, an even bigger word of warning; too much emphasis on measurement will destroy the development of an engaged and inclusive culture. The approach to measurement will depend on both the "type" of culture that is being adopted to align with the society the organization operates within, as well as the level of organizational maturity.

The goal is to reach a state where the core purpose of measures will be to monitor the ongoing sustainability of "the system." If an organization has "the right people on the bus" through effective hiring; has the right people in supervisory positions, and is dealing with individual issues in a collaborative, personal and coaching context, then there will be little need for more "heavy handed" individual assessments; as an example the approach credited to Jack Welch, retired CEO of GE who appeared to suggest that only by identifying and firing the lowest 5% performers each year would leave you with a productive workforce. This engenders fear, not trust.

Measurement might be viewed as snapshots along the journey of development. For hiring, it would be important to know answers about the functioning of the process as follows:

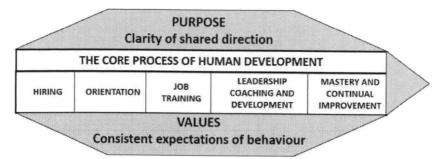

Figure 14 Continuum of development

- On-time hire; people available when needed
- Cycle time from need to hire
- Success rate of hire based on orientation and "job ready"
- Quality of hire - based on # passing selection by stage
- Quality of pool - success as % of total applications

The measures tell us whether the process is working effectively. This then continues with orientation

- On-time completion of orientation
- Orientation evaluation (self-evaluation by individual and then feedback from "leaders")
- % of employees repeating orientation training

The next stage would assess the development of the individual "on the job" from a physical and technical capability; while these are linked to behaviours, they relate most to the technical skills training, physical capabilities, and work environment. These would come from individual self-assessments created by the employee and shared, discussed and agreed with the immediate supervisor (all evaluations would be carried out this way as a process of mutual understanding and development).

- Do you have the working tools and equipment needed for your job?
- Do you have quality concerns related to your work?
- Are you actively involved in problem solving?
- Are you able to collaborate effectively with others?
- Are you able to help develop realistic work targets?
- Is the workload fair and reasonable? Are you able to achieve your work targets?
- Are you involved with work planning and tracking?
- Are you involved in administrative aspects of your job?

The next section would relate to leadership development of both the individual (potential) and the current leader / supervisor. Topics might include:

- Do we all try and make this a great place to work?
- Are you kept aware and involved with changing events?
- Do you have clear expectations of your job and how it fits in with our overall purpose?
- Is your potential being best used in your current position?
- Is there a high level of cooperation in your work group?
- Is there a level of trust in your workgroup?
- Is self-awareness encouraged and supported?
- Are you aware of future opportunities for growth?
- I have a level of freedom to act in my work.
- Rewards for my work are fair.
- Does the company care about me as a person?

Finally, questions related to the organizations ability to create an environment where continuous development, learning and improvement is fostered:

- Are you involved in continuous improvement activity?
- Do you generate ideas for improvement?
- Do you believe your ideas are valued?
- Are your ideas acted upon?
- Are you able to seek out new challenges?
- Is the company prepared for the future?

Trying to obtain answers to the above questions would be easy through a survey but the ability to act on it (the next chapter) would be limited.

Resolving issues that arise from the types of questions being posed to measure and evaluate the culture of the organization, cannot be acted up based on averages. They are individual by individual, work group by work group, section by section, department by department, plant by plant.

In the same way that the underlying values that are established to guide behaviour at the top level will need to be decomposed into meaningful expectations at the plant, department, work group and individual level, so will the action plan necessary to optimize performance.

Remember back to the definition of the organization - using this it is evident that organizations do not improve performance - this only happens through the individual and collective actions of people. To recap, the measures are to assess the way the system is working to enable the optimization of human potential.

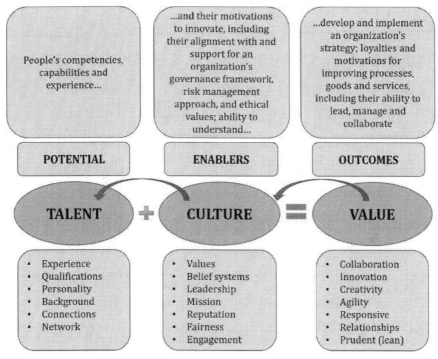

Figure 15 Culture enables talent to create value

Plan for the behaviour - what you want and what you want to be known for. Hire and promote on that basis. Measure how you are doing and then "act" to ensure compliance and improvement.

There is one last measure that there are mixed feelings about, but which can bring significant benefits in the leadership area. Values relate to behaviour, and as was discussed earlier, leadership behaviour is critically important the embedding and sustaining the desired vales and behaviours. For this reason, organizations will use a 360° assessment. While there are generic question sets for a 360° the best approach is to build a set of questions that relate to the expected leadership behaviours. This would include aspects such as demonstrating the values, communications, trust, fairness, openness, respect, involvement, and others. The following is an example using some of the values from the "Is / Is Not" sheet discussed earlier.

"Is" definition	Feedback question
❑ Fostering trust, communication, and inclusiveness	I create an environment of trust I am a good listener I promote inclusiveness
❑ Provide equal opportunity.	I provide equal opportunities I am fair in dealing with others
❑ To listen and to show concern / empathy.	I show empathy for staff concerns
❑ Be consistent in our approach to discipline and rewarding performance.	I am consistent with others I encourage and support staff I reward employees
❑ Set clear guidelines for expected performance and behaviour.	I work with staff to set goals I set clear expectations
❑ Provide a safe workplace - physically, emotionally & mentally.	I provide the equipment required for a safe workplace I support employee needs for a safe workplace I support employee's overall health and well-being
❑ Show care, respect, and acknowledgement of all.	I show care when dealing with others I am respectful of others

The questions used here are specifically designed to assess the degree to which individuals in leadership positions demonstrate the desired qualities. The individual would do their own self-assessment (using the "I" form) and then others - peers, superiors and subordinates would also answer the same questions which would be worded using either "he" or "she").

There is a place for overall surveys as long as the data collected can be identified by work area; if these are used participation of employees must take place both when setting questions and when interpreting the results collected. They need to be administered on a regular basis and contain a limited number of questions.

Another area where data can be collected is from exit interviews. This should be considered whenever a relationship changes - terminations, layoff's, downsizing, transfers. In every situation an individual can reflect on their time in a particular work area and provide valuable feedback.

Organizations should also assess their culture from an external perspective. Input from suppliers, customers, distributors, and others can provide valuable insight. Recent studies by Harvard also indicate that some organizations are tracking "language, phraseology and terminology" used by employees for communications as these can be indicators of underlying feelings about the "reality of the culture". Caution is necessary as although access to much of this data may be legal e.g., company e-mails, using it for such purposes can significantly impact trust.

There are also external sources that can be scanned and assessed, social media as an example. Anything posted publicly about the organization should be tracked and monitored as an indicator. Public websites such as Glassdoor, can provide interesting feedback on both an organizations culture as well as opinions about senior management. There are also emerging AI (Artificial Intelligence) based services, being offered to organizations, that can scan a wide range of data in the marketplace and pick up reputational comments and trends. Again, caution should be exercised both bias, truth, and impact on trust; also remember that this data will reflect a wide range of quality and might best help by illustrating underlying and developing trends.

The "C" - Measurement summary
• The goal of measurement is to assess sustainability of "performance enabling" behaviour.
• Measurement is a continuum of coaching and periodic "state or condition" checking.
• Measurement approaches must cover both "activity" and "outcomes" to cover sustaining activities and results
• Different measures will be needed at each stage of the integrated HR experience.
• Measurement approaches will be both objective and subjective.
• Measures will focus on workgroups and collective behaviour.
• Heavy emphasis must be placed on self-assessments and joint evaluations.
• Surveys can play a role but MUST be aligned with and reflect the anticipated behaviours (e.g., using the "Is" behavioural aspects of the values to ensure operational reality.
• Measures will look at subtle changes and shifts and will underpin strategy through tracking trends.
• Measures will take a "system" approach rather than a focusing on just individual behaviour.
• Humans are always on a "behavioural journey" so progress and responses will be expected to vary by individual.
• Independent exit interviews can yield information on underlying issues and concerns.
• 360° degree leadership assessments can play a key role in sustaining the desired climate being created by individuals in leadership positions.

The "C" Measurement checklist
• Is there a clearly defined understanding of expected values at both leadership levels and others.
• Have the questions and topics for discussion been developed directly from the expected values (especially relative to where the organization is on its journey towards a clearly defined culture)?
• Is the "bias" towards individual self-assessment and coaching at the work group level?
• Are the topics being discussed a reasonable balance between technical skills and capabilities and the expected workplace behaviours?
• Do individuals in leadership roles have the necessary development in both coaching and problem solving to provide this support to employees?
• Is the measurement bias towards "fixing the system" rather than suggesting that the individual is the problem?
• If surveys are used are the questions being developed using employee input (to reduce management bias)?
• Are employees involved in interpretation and analysis of survey feedback to enhance understanding of why people responded this way" and what actions might be required?
• For 360° assessment is information available on each of the individual leaders underlying personality to help identify strengths as well as possible areas for improvement.
• Are the outcomes of all approaches to measurement providing adequate information to direct attention towards both what the problem is and what, specifically is needed to correct it?
• Is there correlation between activity and outcome measures?

7 Act - Use the Information

The purpose of metrics in culture, is to establish "fact based management" using the stated expectations as the base. This applies both for the "task" and for the behaviour. Using and applying effective metrics PLUS the way such data is used, is at the heart of a culture that "acts" rather than "reacts." To think about effective management of a culture one must think about human behaviour in the same way as organizational performance.

The goal is to "shift the curve" of the collective work of everyone and everything involved. Improve every aspect of the business model, especially people, and the performance of the business will improve. No one likes to be singled out or picked on. Many people already know when their performance is sub-par. The job of management is to create a work environment that is trusting so that the truth can be told, and then coach and support those who already know the issues and take other action for those who might be less aware.

Responsibility for action rests in several locations. First, if there are issues in the hiring area including reconciling the organizational values with what is being seen and heard during the hiring process this may suggest a different thing that may need to be addressed:

- The organizational values do not reflect the reality of society.

- The candidates do not believe what they see (reputational issue?)
- Society is changing and the organization is getting out of touch (where the metrics show a declining trend).
- The team addressing face-to-face with candidates is not providing a consistent picture of the company.
- The skill sets being sought is unrealistic.
- The process needs simplification.

Resolving the apparent issues must fall back to the team involved in the process for reflection and analysis. They may need to call on support specialists to help analyse the issues and facilitate potential improvements.

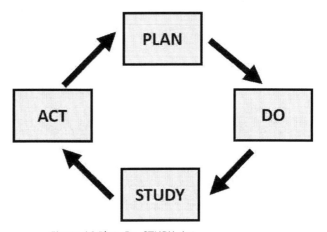

Figure 16 Plan, Do, STUDY, Act

The PDSA version of the familiar continual process is what is used to evaluate the results from metrics. The "Do" is the perform and the actual results being achieved, and the "Study" is the evaluation of information to focus on direct action. This "sub version" is constantly being applied by the organization using the constant accumulation of data about what is happening.

Traditional thinking is that process management and improvement focuses on operational process. However, in a knowledge based, service economy the majority of resources are applied to service processes; these become a major consumer of cash and so financial improvement should come from process improvement. The metrics will inform about the process but like all processes there will be "natural variation."

Using this concept, the metrics for the HR Hiring process must be viewed through the lens of SPC (Statistical Process Control). What is an acceptable level of change before something needs to be investigated? Maybe one set of hiring questions seem more negative but maybe it was snowing on that day and candidates were not just cynical about the company values, they were cynical about everything?

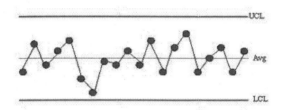

Figure 17 Typical control chart

In this example each plot represents a specific reading or group of readings for a date - as an example the responses from prospective candidate opinions on the company values. As long as the results are within the UCL and LCL (Upper and Lower Control Limits) they would be accepted; however, if they go outside these lines, there would be a review and discussion about what happened on that occasion. NOTE - this is not an SPC course!

For feedback from the one-on-one assessments, that all start with the employee doing a self assessment and then discussing it and obtaining agreement with their immediate supervisor, action again may vary. The big question will be a discussion on "why?" Why did the employee rate something lower than expected? What would the employee suggest as a solution? What input does the supervisor have? Is this a trend that the supervisor has seen from other in the workgroup and if so, what does the supervisor propose to do as a suggested action? How will they involve the employees in the solution? What other help is needed? Through this discussion most points should be resolved. If there are clearly one of more issues that cannot be resolved, then there could be an appeal to involve others in the discussion. The goal is resolution and consensus.

While assessments are done at least annually these are supported by day by day week by week open communications and support from both the supervisor and others. One example used in manufacturing is the ability of the employee to "stop the line" and point out a problem that must be resolved before starting work again. There is no reason that this approach could not be used in any processes within other organizations. Tracking the number of times these "stops" occur can also be another useful measure to assess both employee commitment to quality as well as engagement. Again, these numbers would be tracked on control charts and "out of control" (i.e., more frequent "stops" than planned) would be investigated by the team.

The leadership evaluation using the 360° assessment would initially be discussed with the immediate superior as part of their evaluation; however, the goal would, once again focus on "why did people answer this way" and "why do you think this was their impression?" If there seems to be some key differences, then once again the individual could ask for help and support in understanding the input and this might take place in the form of a focus group. In extreme circumstances, one or more third parties might be asked to facilitate these discussions. (It would be hoped this this does not happen based on effective hiring and promotion).

In all cases, every individual would jointly develop their own unique learning and development plan for the future, and this would include coaching and support from the immediate team leader.

Some of the more general, organization wide measures including data collected externally might be considered "strategic intelligence." Again, these should be evaluated and treated as trends and indicators as they will usually be "system wide" and a challenge to link to specific action. How organizations respond to data being collected is, in itself an action that will impact trust; the goal should be to make everything that is being collected public knowledge, and create a willingness to receive feedback and ideas about both "why we are getting these results" and potentially "what should we do about it?"

Finally, the collective intelligence gained from every piece of information around culture should form a key part of feedback into the next planning cycle. Changes that follow will not be limited to "people issue" but will cover the purpose aspect, because, as the culture "check" stage demonstrated, some of the responses relate to the impact of work aspects - understanding the purpose, having the right tools, being able to manage the workload etc.

The "A" Act summary
<ul><li>People / behavioural measures, tracking and action must be equally important as task / process.</li><li>The outcome from the "Check" stage must be adequate to link to action.</li><li>Many activity measures will demonstrate aspects of process performance and "control limits" should be established to guide when responses are required.</li><li>Action must be affirmative (on track), corrective (not on track but intent correct) or strategic (not on track and unlikely to be achieved or possible).</li><li>On track reinforces approaches currently being used</li><li>Corrective requires operational changes such as process changes, leadership improvements / clarification, or other actions</li><li>Strategic requires a connection back to planning so as to change or modify the intent or approach to execution.</li><li>Where possible corrective action plans must be driven by the employees own suggestions and commitments.</li><li>Actions taken must themselves reflect the underlying values (e.g., trust, fairness, engagement etc.)</li><li>Psychometrics and other tools can provide significant help in determining actions required especially for those in leadership roles.</li></ul>

The "A" Act checklist
• Are all measurement results actionable?
• Is all feedback from measures actioned?
• Is responsibility for action seen as an individual leadership action where needed rather than an HR issue?
• Does HR provide an underpinning supportive role for managers and leaders?
• Does HR support employee "corrective action" with supportive resources such as EAR, EAP etc.
• Is there broad communication both of expectations and of actual broad based organizational progress?
• Do employees take a lead position in improvement and self development?
• Is there broad engagement of corrective action when common issues are revealed?
• Are action plans focused on removal of performance obstacles and other tangible enablers?
• Is there a process in place for escalation, coaching and support when managers / leaders encounter challenges in arriving at performance consensus?

Corporate Culture

8 Understanding people and Maturity

8.1 The importance of understanding human behaviour

One of the greatest challenges in establishing and sustaining a desired culture is that it about human beings. While one can establish expectations and try to hire, promote, and evaluate based on these expectations, people are not always predictable! Additionally, everybody comes with natural underlying tendencies and the organization hires "the whole person." Who we are and how we act is complex?

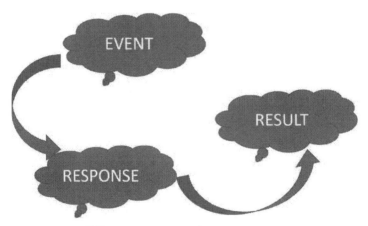

Figure 18 Human response mechanism

Individually, events initiate a response which generates a result. These results can be instinctive and reactive, which will reflect underlying belief systems, values, and principles; they can also be "reflective" and based on some level of consideration. Most reactive responses are driven emotionally - but not always. The result we get is partly in our control if "we stop and think about it." What is important is that human beings are "conditioned" to respond in some way.

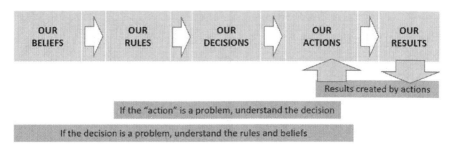

Figure 19 The generation of results

Our responses to events are driven by one or more actions that are driven by conscious or sub-conscious decision making. The decisions we make are drawn from a combination of rules and beliefs. These include our own unique personality, our life experiences, and our emotional stability and well being. What ends up in the workplace and interacts with others is "our whole self."

There can be several possible reasons, if the results that are being seen and the actions that drive them are inconsistent with expectations. This is where organizational culture is so critical; it is an approach to define a common baseline for decision making to create the actions and results that are desired. To *assume* that people will act in a certain way is risky and so hiring, promotion and evaluation are all important aspects of reducing the risk of unexpected actions and results. So, step one is to define, share and constantly reinforce expected behaviour.

Secondly, it is important to realize that events happen in people's lives that affect what might be called their "normal" behaviour. A great employee suddenly starts being "not so great." What happened? Did this person change overnight? Probably not - something may have happened to them in their personal (or even work) life that has impacted their normal rules and decision making. This can be stress, conflict, tension, emotional issues, dietary changes, loss of a loved one, children leaving home, behavioural issues, societal or community problems, fear of getting older, fear of money problems, threats, and many, many more. Organizations cannot ignore these nor should they try to pressure the individual to "leave their personal issues at home."

This is why people in leadership positions must always be aware of changes in behaviour that are "un-characteristic" of the individual; they also need to demonstrate some level of care, empathy and understanding in working with the employee to deal with the issues. There also need to be human resource systems and resources to help support individuals who face these "life events" which impact their performance at work. Care also needs to be taken that the workplace itself is not the cause of the problems; it is a well known fact that mental illness has become a growing problem and, in many cases, caused by increased pressure in the workplace. So, factors external to work can cause changes in behaviour that may seem inconsistent with the culture.

Thirdly, the organization needs to make sure that undesired results are not being caused by inappropriate actions just because the individual "did not know" how to respond or what was expected. This is why coaching and supporting employee development is such an important part of developing and reinforcing the desired behaviour. This is another key strategic reason why an organizational culture is so critical as it forms a consistent baseline of moving towards a consistent and sustainable base for behaviour through the constant learning and reinforcement based on the reality of every individual's contribution.

Next, is to realize that even "the right people" may come with "baggage" that may not change the individual underlying personality but may alter their "learned responses." This is again why coaching and supporting are important. As an example, some people may tend to be biased towards being naturally collaborative but have experienced negative results from an environment where there is both little trust and is extremely competitive, and as a result had many of their ideas "stolen" by others and were not recognized for their contribution and capability. In this way their "belief" has been modified and they are downplaying a natural tendency because of what has happened.

As a result, they may tend to become less collaborative and more "self-centred" and unwilling to share. The "natural person" is still there, and it is the role of the workplace to create an environment where people's natural talents are supported, encouraged, and allowed to flourish. This is where creating an environment of trust is so foundational. However, it will not happen overnight; supportive actions need to be repeated and reinforced so that "beliefs" can be changed or at least the "barriers" removed. Beliefs are a key driver of decisions and actions.

Finally, the big challenge; assuming the hiring, promotion and evaluation processes narrow down the risk of getting "the wrong people on the bus" - even the right people have unique personalities that will result in natural tendencies that in some areas may compliment the expected behavioural values. Organizations that help employees "self reflect" and become more aware and accepting of their own unique personality will often benefit because the self-awareness leads to a recognition that others also have unique personalities; not good, not bad - simply different. There are a number of inspirational quotes that reinforce the importance of self-awareness:

- Knowing yourself is the beginning of all wisdom. *Aristotle*
- To thine own self be true. *Shakespeare*

One might be tempted to be sceptical of being able to do this; many organizations are full of people who spend a lot of their time "acting out of character" or "play acting" because that is what they think is expected. Here is an important life learning relative to organizational culture:

"I've found it's ever so clear when people are working out of alignment with their core values. It can be a miserable and even devastating experience. Interestingly, unhappy professionals often know something is terribly wrong, but can't pinpoint exactly what is making them feel so disrespected, undervalued, and unappreciated. In many cases, it's a serious clash in values." *"In several jobs, I felt that my employers' behavior, mission and culture clashed fiercely with what I held to be good, true and respectable."*

This quote is from a Forbes article by Kathy Caprino, a Career Coach and it illustrates the situation of "the wrong fit." Unfortunately, people often "learn to live with it" in spite of it being bad for the individual and the organization. Another career coach, Jane Jackson states the following in a blog she published on LinkedIn:

"Often it starts with a feeling that something doesn't 'feel right' or it goes against the grain. You may feel that what is expected of you is wrong. The problem in this case, is that you may have to behave in a certain way in order to keep your job, or keep the peace, or avoid conflict or confrontation."

Aligning individuals with the values of the organization is good for both parties but can be a challenge which starts with creating a trusting environment:

- Honesty and transparency make you vulnerable. Be honest and transparent anyway. — *Mother Theresa*
- The privilege of a lifetime is to become who you truly are. – *Carl Jung*

There is whole profession centred around helping organizations develop their employees through the use of tools that help individuals understand about themselves and about those they work with. We have suggested that "open communications" is an important organizational attribute but something as simple as this can change based on a person's personality. Here is an example of a "learning" that came out of one such tool related to how people communicate. Each person's preference was identified:

Name	Communicating with me, I like you to...	Communicating with me, I do not like it when you...	I offer our high performing team
JCD	Take time and care in putting new ideas into action, but this does not stop me from standing up for new ideas where I can see their merit. I get a lot from talking to people about things that I find interesting and feel enthusiastic about.	Rush a debate about something important. I feel that a rash decision should be avoided if only a little extra time was spent discussing the issue. Yet those who become indecisive under pressure can be frustrating for me.	I am known for saying what needs to be said. This can be an important skill when a team is faced with a difficult situation where others may try and stay away from contentious issues.

From the above we see that JCD clearly has a style of both giving and receiving communications. Without knowing this about JCD others may communicate "naturally" in a different manner. Here was RM's choices:

Name	Communicating with me, I like you to...	Communicating with me, I don't like it when you...	I offer our high performing team
RM	I like it when people can support their arguments rationally. I like to discuss ways in which theories can be transformed into workable processes.	In a discussion I dislike things becoming over-complicated when a simple solution would suffice.	Other team members appreciate me for the clarity of my reasoning. When I explain something, I go through it step-by-step in a logical fashion.

One can see in the case of RM they do not want to get over complicated - yet JCD does not want to rush the conversation. Could be a point of conflict? Knowing this would allow each of them to understand how to communicate more effectively with each other, and also make each of them aware of their own style when communicating with others - and become more aware of their potential reaction?

The underlying investment in understanding unique personality is especially important in those in leadership roles. Knowing their own unique personality and how that may differ from others in their workgroup builds a foundation for effectively working together.

For leaders it may also open up an understanding of their own leadership style which emanated from their personality. There is no right or wrong personality for leaders - yet some lead by inspiration, some by their personal drive, some by attention to detail and analysis and others through their ability to work collaboratively and build relationships.

We started off by saying organizational culture is "about the way we do things around here." It is about how people communicate and interact - and a key part of this is common language and shared understanding. One mistake that reduces the effectiveness of efforts to build a culture is to switch providers of tools and services especially in the field of human resource management and in particular in tools related to behaviours and personalities. We also stated that key aspects of building a culture include hiring, development, leadership, workgroup development

While there are many providers in the field, one that the author has personal knowledge of and strongly recommends is a UK based company called Lumina Learning. Lumina has a suite of products developed by their owner and founder Dr. Stewart Desson that are based on solid research and built around consistency of thinking. Compare their list of products to the key steps in building a culture:

Product	Where it fits in culture development
Spark	Foundation tool for everyone that provides a common framework for understanding personality, based on an individual's strengths and developmental areas. Spark measures and reports on 72 personality qualities indicating underlying (real), everyday (conditioned) and extended (stressed) behaviours.
Select	Recruitment tool based on Spark understanding of personality and comparing this for a "fit" with the organizations unique culture. Helps select get "the right people on the bus" and identify opportunities for development.
Leader	Using the same qualities as Spark this tool allows the individual to understand the link between their personality and leadership style and this can then be compared to the culture, so as to identify strengths and development areas.
Team	Team investigates the team's own perspective of its character as well as how other people view it. Participants co-create greater team awareness and understanding, learning to value each member's unique contribution. Again, based on same qualities as Spark.
Sales	The Lumina Sales Portrait assesses how an individual's personal qualities will affect the way they are likely to perform at each stage of the sales cycle. Valuable assist in relationship development and management aspect of culture relative to 3rd party relationships.
Emotion	Complementary to Spark and related to emotional aspect of behaviour. Lumina Emotion teaches how to manage personality effectively to suit changing contextual demands, whatever an individual's personal traits may be.

The understanding and terminology are common throughout the portfolio of products so that sharing and communications is eased and assisted. The foundational product that would be used on every member of the organization would then be the common building block for all other development areas.

While other products may be available that are consistent and broad enough to cover the key aspects of culture building, Lumina presents the type of "founding specification" that an organization should seek if it is serious about a strategic investment in building its' human potential and capability.

8.2 The Mature Organization

One outcome of an effective culture is an organization where people are seen as being central to success. There is a concept, developed by The Maturity Institute in the UK that reflects and complements the suggestions that have been discussed about culture, and who have also developed a "whole system" critical performance indicator to evaluate how well the organization is doing on this journey.

While financial performance remains an important indicator of whole system performance, it often fails to assess the underlying health of the non-financial components of the value creation system. The MI system, named OMINDEX is based on research of key success factors in evaluating the health, risk, and sustainability of the whole "business system entity." While historically financial heath has been used to assess an organization as a "going concern" this is inadequate for human centric organizations that are prevalent in todays economy.

The Institute developed 32 questions contained for its organizational assessment, that is performed by trained analysts to ensure consistent application and interpretation. Based on a review of these questions (publicly available) it would appear that 14 are specifically relevant to the development of an effective culture and another 14 cover a combination of

Purpose and Values, leaving only 4 questions that focus on Purpose alone. This would seem to suggest that the model for an effective business in the 21st century requires an equal combination of both clarity of Purpose PLUS clarity of expected behaviours? Below is an extract of the assessment showing questions that would seem to be relevant to culture:

#	Maturity assessment question for rating
5	Governance: does anyone on the Board of one of its committees or the Executive hold specific responsibility for human governance?
6	Trust: to what extent are the leadership and management team trusted by customers, employees, and other key stakeholders?
7	Values: have at least three core values been expressed by the organization?
9	Value potential: to what extent does the organization seek to maximize the value it generates from all of its human capital - both directly employed and within its supply chain and wider society?
14	Culture: what evidence is there that the Board recognizes and understands the importance of organizational culture and is it being monitored effectively?
16	Business planning: to what extent are improvements in the organization's capability in human capital management specifically factored into its current business plan?
20	Innovation system: does the organization have a system to measure the rate of innovation of the entire workforce (including suppliers) and, if so, to what extent is it applied?
22	Learning & knowledge: to what extent is this a learning organization that continuously and expeditiously aims to acquire and apply knowledge, expertise, and experience to continuously create more value and reduce risk?
23	Identifying the specific value impact of human capital: to what extent are business improvements based in linking human capital to the value variables OCRQE?

#	Maturity assessment question for rating
24	Return on human capital: has the organization adopted a discipline of linking human capital directly to financial returns by completing an ROI calculation?
25	Cooperation: to what extent is the organization characterized by willing, active, and enthusiastic cooperation all the way from leaders and managers to the most junior job roles and to suppliers?
26	People risk: to what extent does the organization have a comprehensive system for measuring and assessing the current level of human capital management risk within the organization?
27	Remuneration and reward: has the organization adopted, and does it adhere to, a clear set of key principles to underpin its remuneration and reward policy and link it directly to stakeholder value?
31	Decision making environment: to what extent would you describe high-level decision making in the organization as collegiate?

Further information is available from The Maturity Institute whose website contains background information and case studies on their research. One of the main reasons for covering this approach is that it is used in the case study in the next chapter as an example of a tool that can be used to assess organizational health and risk, in an environment where values and behaviour are increasing important.

People and Maturity - summary
• People act and make decisions based on underlying beliefs and values
• If you want to change behaviour that drives decision making you need to understand "why" a person made that choice.
• These beliefs and values are a combination of "natural personality" and learned behaviours.
• Some people will not "fit" with the expected behaviours which reinforces the importance of selection.
• To change behaviour there is a need to both define / communicate expectations and to coach and develop.
• Different people, while sharing "values" may have different styles which will impact areas such as communications as well as approaches to "enabling motivation."
• People are impacted by events outside work and so changes in work behaviour may be externally driven.
• For people to optimize their contribution there must be a climate of acceptance of "uniqueness" and a climate of trust.
• Organizational maturity develops when human potential and capability is fully enabled a strategic value creating resource (not a cost).
• A mature organization is one where the ability to be "human centric" has been developed to the highest level of strategic importance.
• Leadership is a key enabler of Maturity starting at the highest levels (with Purpose and Values having equal importance).
• There is a high level of consistency between the drivers of a "managed culture" and the factors assessed to determine organizational maturity.

People and Maturity checklist
• Is there any assessment tool used at the interview stage to increase the probability of a good behavioural fit?
• Is this assessment tool independent and objective and free of bias?
• Is there a process to evaluate personality against values to assess risk and fit?
• Are mistakes treated as performance and discipline issues or are they investigated for root "systemic" cause?
• Are tools used to support hiring and development at individual and group level consistent in terminology?
• Are development tools consistent and are they used as part of a continuous process (i.e., supporting a journey not an event?)
• Is leadership development supported by an understanding of personal traits that impact style and approach?
• Does internal communications training and development embrace different listening and speaking styles based on personality?
• Does the organization have any way, other than financial results, to assess "while system" performance (i.e., the level at which integration is successfully creating value)?
• Is there an integrated risk assessment approach and if so, does it include a detailed assessment of behavioural risks?

9 Poor Culture Cost Study

By this time some may be asking why? Building a culture looks like a big deal? It is going to take a long time. Yes - but NOT having an effective culture can be a major risk. As was identified earlier, reliance on a "clean bill of health" and assurance of a "going concern" cannot be assured through a clean financial audit.

This chapter reflects an earlier study designed to demonstrate the cost of a poor culture; in many cases there is enhanced risk, but the problems only show up when there are surprises. The study focused on the financial aspects of culture in three areas - "financial surprises," "inefficiencies and hidden costs," and, "missed opportunities."

> Note: this case study uses publicly available information at the time. It has been used for illustrative purposes only and makes no judgement on the actions taken or results.

9.1 Financial Performance and Culture

Culture is not a new issue for accountants or those involved in corporate governance and risk management; as an example, the current CoSo assessment framework for assessing internal controls – the normal basis of defining what risks need to be addressed, starts with considering "the tone at the top." This importance on the role of leadership affirms the importance of human behaviour on organizational risk. However, the importance of human behaviour has never been more critical and there are number of drivers for this increased impact:

- Mobility and communications – different peoples from different backgrounds - upon which their personal values are developed, are working together in the same organizations across national boundaries.
- Demographics – never have so many different generations been working together in the workplace each having differing values that drive their beliefs and behaviours.
- Globalization and competitiveness – increased trade flows and the emergence of low cost producers has increased global competition and significantly impacted the challenge of competitiveness; to meet this organizations must make decisions and respond faster than ever before.
- Growth in the service economy – organizations depend heavily on intellectual capital and knowledge management – and to do this increasingly delegate decision making to a greater number of individuals than in a traditional hierarchy.

Finally, to complicate matters involving human behaviour still further, research is now showing us that human decision making is not as rational as once was believed; this has profound impacts for professions such as economics which was built upon a basis of human rationality. We also know that far from being "generic" in thinking and personality, people are quite different and will act in different ways when faced with certain stimulations.

This evolution on business reality and human behaviours might – or probably should, raise fear in the hearts of accountants, investors, and boards of directors. There are all sorts of different and possibly irrational people out there, who all think differently and are running around making day to day decisions in their organizations – especially since these behavioural aspects apply equally to senior managers and "C" suite executives! No wonder that culture is becoming recognized as something that is important in organizational performance. The important question though is "does it really matter?"

9.1.1   Organizational maturity and culture

For the purposes of this paper, it is being assumed that a mature organization is one that has developed a culture that positively impacts operating performance. Likewise, a lower level of maturity would suggest a "less than optimum" use of organizational resources and capabilities? Organizational maturity can be expressed on a scale developed by The Maturity Institute and used to evaluate organizations as shown below:

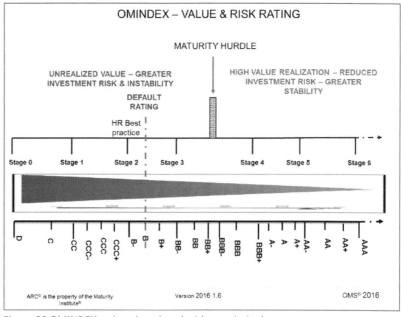

Figure 20 OMINDEX rating chart (used with permission)

The various stages depict the levels of organizational maturity and the ratings, shown at the bottom of the chart (from AAA to D) translate scoring from OMINDEX assessments, into ratings, using a scale comparable to that used by financial analysts such as S&P and Moody's. The lower the rating, the greater the potential risk in the organizations ability to create and sustain value; the default rating shows statistically where a normal distribution would place an average organization (the mean). Most assessments of organizational performance risk are currently heavily weighted to financial reporting and current approaches to financial reporting provide limited help to understanding the financial risk associated with low maturity and poor culture.

There are three key risks that impact financial performance related to lower maturity and poor culture – the problem is that in almost all situations current financial reporting does a poor job of highlight such risks and when it is reflected it is often after the event; these three aspects are:

- Financial surprises – unanticipated impacts on financial performance that occur due to control failures and unanticipated behaviour (examples would be legal and regulatory fines and penalties as well as other actions).
- Buried impacts of current lower or poor financial performance which come from restraints on value creation – lower output, higher costs, lower revenues and lower quality of products and services.
- Lost opportunities to enhance value which come from opportunities to increase output, lower costs, increase revenues and enhance quality.

Financial surprises are typically unanticipated, have a negative impact on earnings and will usually reduce organizational value. They do considerable damage to an organization brand and reputation and can cause both significant fines and even legal prosecution; they also impact and usually reduce market value.

The second situation, buried impacts caused by "sub optimization" which results in higher operating costs per unit of output, are often not visible and are buried within the existing expenses; while performance benchmarking might indicate opportunity for improvement the excess costs are not clearly reported or understood – it's just "what it is." Often, as a result of these perceived excess costs, organizations resort to short term cost cutting measures like layoffs which might have short term benefits but in the longer term do little to enhance cultural maturity – and often cause deterioration in morale and other areas. In effect these responses negatively impact corporate culture

The third area of "lost opportunity" is the most strategically critical. Most organizations develop performance improvement budgets but rarely is the question asked, *"how much better could performance be, if everything and everyone was operating as part of a fully effective, aligned and holistic system?"* It is interesting that when the "Cost of Poor Quality" was developed as an approach to understanding the impact of poor quality on financial performance, the following definition was developed and is still used today:

Total Quality Costs represent the difference between the actual cost of a product or service and what the reduced cost would be if there were no possibility of sub-standard service, failure of products, or defects in their manufacture."

Principles of Quality Costs, 3rd edition 1999, Jack Campanella and ASQ Quality Costs Committee, Quality Press.

"Whole system" proponents have been exploring "optimum performance" for years; the "Theory of Constraints (TOC)" was one such approach that demonstrated the potential improvements available from those who had moved to a more "systems thinking" framework[1]. Results

---

[1] Quick guide to Theory of Constraints http://www.tocinstitute.org/theory-of-constraints.html

claimed from addressing underlying system problems included significant increases in performance.

On time delivery	⬆	**60%**
Revenues increases	⬆	68%
Profit increases	⬆	82%
Inventory reduction	⬇	50%
Cycle time reduction	⬇	66%

Figure 21 Typical improvements from applying TOC

This holistic or whole systems thinking is core to maturity and the creation of a positive culture and as will be demonstrated can significantly reduce organizational risk and enhance operating performance. These two factors combined enhance both organizational competitiveness and sustainability.

The three issues of surprises, sub-optimization, and lost opportunities, can be depicted as risks inherent in the current approach to business operations – which can be complemented by the scoring on the OMINDEX rating using the following example:

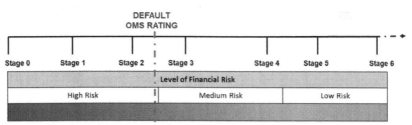

Figure 22 Risk overlay to OMINDEX rating

High and medium risk organizations have a greater potential for unexpected financial events; these should decline as the organization matures (i.e., the OMINDEX rating improves); they also have almost no recognition of existing opportunities to add value through removing inbuilt inefficiencies or innovation. Medium and low risk organizations start to recognize the hidden costs within existing operations and remove these thus adding to profitability and enhancing value creation; low risk organizations have embedded continual improvement and are likely to become increasingly innovative and creative thus continuing to increase value creation capability and become more competitive.

9.2   Challenge 1 – Lowering the risk of surprises

Every organization has a culture that defines the way people think and act; the problem for many organizations is that culture is not something that has been managed but has evolved over time. Of special concern is that cultures can change from being positive to negative based on the demonstrated actions of those in leadership positions. More challenging is that if individual managers and leaders behave in a different way based on different values, then organizational culture becomes very confusing to employees as to how they should behave.

It is the problem of either unknown or unmanaged cultures that carry the greatest risk for surprises. Some organizations have ethics policies or codes of conduct, training programs and policies and procedures; many have well defined processes and may even be ISO 9001 certified for process effectiveness but in reality, all of these are of no value, if people don't understand how to behave in "the white spaces[2]" when decisions are based on judgement.

Probably one of the most obvious "surprise" costs relative to a poor culture is demonstrated by the financial services industry; between 2011 and 2015 research from public domain information indicates that a list of the top twenty International banks who had the most significant records of fines and penalties paid £186.12 billion and were carrying further provisions of £66.13 billion for a total impact on earnings of £252.25 billion[3]

---

[2] "Managing in the White Spaces" Geary Rummler and Alan Brache
[3] Research by CCP Research Foundation

(US $403.6 Billion) To this can be added the prior "societal impact" of bail outs from various national governments; in the US alone the official number was about $700 billion but broader based assessments[4] put the numbers much higher with $4.6 trillion paid out and a total commitment that can be up to $16.8 trillion.

Other examples of financial impacts of behaviour could include fines levied by the US SEC under the Foreign Corrupt Practices Act[5] in 2016 alone on 24 companies (International and US) of $3.4 billion. Other examples for "corporate failures" in areas like environmental conduct would include $6 billion in administrative, civil judicial penalties and criminal fines by the EPA in 2016 alone not counting the $14.7 billion agreed by Volkswagen for the "emissions scandal."

Fines for either illegal behaviour or non-compliance with regulations and standards occur on a global basis – even the US fines quoted above in some cases covered international operations whose securities were traded in the US and identified operational issues in many other countries. These fines can be significant in terms of income; research done by David McCandless back in 2012 showed what percentage of reported income some selected fines amounted to – here is an example:

Year	Company	US $ Fines 2005 – 2012 in $M	Annual US $M income using 2011	Fines as % of 7 year income
2012	Glaxo Smith Kline	$3,000	$8,200	37%
2012	Barclays	$450	$9,100	5%
2010	BP	$34,000	$30,600	110%
2009	Eli Lilly	$1,420	$4,300	33%
2009	Pfizer	$2,300	$8,600	27%

---

[4] See "The Big Bank Bailout," Mike Collins, Forbes Magazine, July 2014
[5] https://www.sec.gov/spotlight/fcpa/fcpa-cases.shtml

While the numbers are significant one could either see them as having a major impact on business – especially BP, yet for the others such as Barclays that is only 5% of seven years income its almost just "a cost of doing business." However, accepting this would have a significant impact on what employees see as "acceptable behaviour?" The challenge appears widespread as the following list[6] shows although it seems that banks, pharmaceutical companies, technology, and equipment area all prominent? This would tend to support the argument that as the economy has become more knowledge based, the risk of behavioural problems has escalated:

Year	Company	Fine in US $ M	Reason
2013	JP Morgan	$4,500	Sold toxic backed mortgage securities
2013	Banks (13 group action)	$9,300	Foreclosed on paid homes and charged illegal fees
2013	HSBC	$1,900	Laundered money for cartels and terrorists
2013	Johnson & Johnson	$2,200	Promoted unsafe drug use
2012	GlaxoSmithKline	$3,000	Misbranded drugs, bribed doctors, lied about prices
2009	Pfizer	$2,300	Misbranded drugs and bribed doctors
2008	Siemens	$1,600	Bribed officials for contracts
2005	AOL	$2,400	Lied about its revenues

Figure 23 Examples of corporate fines

While a smaller number, GM was fined $1M by the SEC over ignition switch problems that apparently killed at least 124 people (small price to

---

[6] Analysis from https://curiousmatic.com/13-largest-penalties-corporations-paid-fraud-corruption-lies/

pay) on top of at least $595M that the company paid out to victims[7]. CEO responses to these fines are interesting; GM CEO Mary Barra told the House Energy and Commerce Subcommittees she is aiming *"...to correct a culture that has displayed a pattern of incompetence and neglect"* which links the problem right back to behaviour but seems to "leave hanging" the role of leadership? Why did people act in a way that was either unethical or illegal?

As can be seen, the costs associated with "surprises" can be significant and have both financial and reputational impacts; at worst they can lead to collapse of a whole sector such as the financial "meltdown" in 2008 – 2010. Financial reporting informed investors about these issues after the fact.

Could investors have been better prepared for these risks? If one looks at the financial services industry, not every bank participated in the problems that led to the collapse; what was the difference – were the other banks more prudent? Was their culture more "risk adverse?" Did every employee understand where the line was beyond which they could not go in decision making?

If we drill down further, is it possible to say that some of the banks approach to hiring and compensation, was more driven by hiring the right people with the "right values" and compensating employees and executives in a way that did not encourage undesired behaviour? Was there an orientation program? Was it effective? Was the whistle blower program effective? Was there a greater level of trust, communication, collaboration, and cooperation within the bank? How are leaders selected, developed, managed, and compensated?

These are all features of the maturity and culture with which the organization is managed. If investors don't have visibility into their

---

[7]   USA   Today   http://www.usatoday.com/story/money/cars/2017/01/18/general-motors-securities-and-exchange-commission-sec-ignition-switch/96717570/

organization's maturity, they have little protection against surprises that reduce earnings and deplete value and, at worst void their investment completely.

9.3   Challenge 2 – Identifying and removing the buried costs

Existing financial reporting provides limited insight into the reasons for existing costs; for external users, costs are aggregated at an extremely high level such as operating expenses, which might then be analyzed by cost of product and services, SG&A (Sales, General and Administrative) and depreciation and amortization; even internally costs tend to be reported "by department, by type of expense."

This approach often leads to reinforcing the belief that "the workforce is the largest cost" and therefore if performance is to be enhanced costs must be reduced. Interestingly in many public financial reports the total "cost" of the workforce is not published. The question should always be "why are the costs as high as they are? What is driving the demand for resources?"

Financial reporting has been a barrier for understanding opportunities for change in the past. When quality management was being recognized as a key issue for business, particularly in the 1970's in North America, many CEO's couldn't see the value or benefits from "investing" in quality management "systems." Very often the rationale was given that better quality would improve customer satisfaction but rarely were quality practitioners able to convince CEO's that not only would better quality save money, *but the absence of it was also already costing the organization significantly higher expenses*. (One quality leader at the time coined the phrase "...hidden gold in the mine.")

It was only when people like the late Phil Crosby in his book "Quality is Free" demonstrated the benefits by dispelling the myth that improving quality would cost money and focused on the "unseen opportunity" did CEO's start to come around. His "stages of maturity" in management approaches to quality demonstrated the problem especially when metrics do not show the existing costs being incurred:

Maturity stage	Description	Management understanding and attitude	Cost of quality as % of sales	
			Reported	Actual
1	Uncertainty	No comprehension of quality as a management tool; tend to blame quality departments for quality problems	Unknown	20.0%
2	Awakening	Recognizes that quality management may be of value but not willing to provide money or time to make it happen	3.0%	18.0%
3	Enlightenment	While going through quality improvement program learn more about quality management; becoming supportive and helpful	8.0%	12.0%
4	Wisdom	Participating; understand absolutes of quality management. Recognize their personal role in continuing emphasis	6.5%	8.0%
5	Certainty	Consider quality management an essential part of the company system.	2.5%	2.5%

Figure 24 Stages of Maturity based on quality concepts

When quality was initially identified as a strategic issue, many organizations were operating at stage 1 or 2 – not realizing that buried in their costs was a possible opportunity to enhance performance by 18 – 20% of revenues. Almost no financial reporting was showing this as it was buried in the existing cost of doing business.

The same has been true of lean / six sigma initiatives; nobody told GE or Motorola that they would save billions of dollars in expenses – but that is what happened. Six Sigma is an approach to improve process performance so that it is almost defect free: 6 Sigma being 3.4 defects per million items, actions, or operations. Typically, organizations have not applied a structured process design activity operate as between 3 and 4 Sigma or at an excess cost estimated to be between 14% and 24% of revenues. The statistics relative to "6 Sigma" are as follows:

Sigma level	Defect level per million	Yield % (good)	Approximate hidden cost as % of revenues
1	691,462	31%	Unknown
2	308,538	69%	Unknown
3	66,807	93.3%	24%
4	6,210	99.38%	14%
5	233	99.99966%	9%
6	3.4 defects	99.9999981%	4%

Figure 25 Process cost impact of defect levels

Quality America reinforced the importance of process improvement in comments about apply the concept:

> For non-Six Sigma companies, these costs are often extremely high. Companies operating at three or four sigma typically spend between 25 and 40 percent of their revenues fixing problems. This is known as the cost of quality, or more accurately the cost of poor quality. Companies operating at Six Sigma typically spend less than 5 percent of their revenues fixing problems. The dollar cost of this gap can be huge. General Electric estimates that the gap between three or four sigma and Six Sigma was costing them between $8 billion and $12 billion per year.
>
> *Quality America Inc.*
> http://qualityamerica.com/LSS-Knowledge-

What was learned in applying 6 Sigma is that there MUST be employee involvement and engagement.

What are these buried costs and where are they? Some may be visible, but the majority are considered part of existing operating expenses. Using information published from studies[8] on improvements related to organizational culture we can identify the following:

#	Benefits observed	Where the negative impact is hidden today
1	10% higher customer ratings	Higher sales and support costs (e.g. call centres) to service higher levels of complaints, problems, customer turnover, returns and time spent when problems are escalated
2	22% higher profitability	Current costs higher due to discounting and credits; losses from employee productivity from lower morale; lower responsiveness to innovation, problem solving and continual improvement; slower cycle times; employees don't "go the extra mile"
3	21% productivity improvement	Current labour costs higher relative to output; problems remain unresolved; supervisors ignore employee ideas; suggestions for improvement are unaddressed; employee ideas for machine improvements ignored; maintenance downtime higher; suppliers unwilling to share improvement ideas; higher sick leave / absenteeism; employees work in silos and fail to collaborate, communicate and share ideas
4	37% lower absenteeism	Currently buried in labour costs which translate into higher costs / unit of output; higher temporary staffing costs; customer penalties from unplanned delivery delays; quality problems from using untrained staff to fill in
5	25% lower turnover	Higher hiring and training costs; larger proportion of employees lower on the "learning curve" so output lower; excessive supervisor time spent on hiring / discipline problems
6	28% lower shrinkage	Currently wastage and losses written off as higher cost of sales; can also impact time spent on inventory counts and analysis
7	48% lower safety accidents and issues	Higher absenteeism for sick days (higher temp staffing / union pay adjustments / overtime costs); indirect negative impact on customers (services not provided)
8	41% lower defect rates	May show up as excessive scrap or rework costs but in many cases buried within existing operating costs when work is repeated to

Figure 26 Potential opportunities from buried costs

[8] Wall Street Journal October 2011 citing Felps, Terence and Byington

Successful organizations have used the Cost of Poor Quality (COPQ) framework developed by The American Society of Quality to "extract" the underlying costs and make then visible. Simplistically the approach involves the identification of activities and events that occur in the organization that drive the consumption of resources, but which, if everything was working effectively should not happen.

A similar approach could be applied to the identification of existing operating costs that are being impacted by key risk areas in human governance and human capital management. The following table is extracted from research the Maturity Institute undertook, that identified key areas of risk that can have an impact on operational effectiveness and thus costs.

Risk area	Nature of risk	Examples of operational costs impact
Systemic disconnection: reward and value outcomes	Rewards for senior executives through to management and staff do not relate to value and encourages other outcomes.	Higher absenteeism from safety issues; encourages higher turnover through poor morale which drives higher hiring costs; increase losses / theft; sales /support costs increase caused by focusing on financial returns more than client satisfaction (legal bias vs. relationship); higher overtime costs
Knowledge and learning failures	Failure to use internal knowledge; Inability to learn from mistakes	Higher process costs due to defects and repeated errors; less process improvement; problems hidden and not resolved; higher call centre costs (repeated calls / problems not solved); consultants used vs. employee driven improvements
Supply / value chain failures	Weak oversight driven by cost rather than value	Lower product costs being more than offset by higher administrative costs due to paperwork defects, rework, failures to deliver on time and others; savings not passed on by vendors
Target and goal setting	Excessive, meaningless and/or conflicting performance targets & KPIs drive adverse outcomes	Excess reporting / admin time; more meetings vs. voluntary collaboration and cooperation; workplace conflict / stress causing higher sick leave; excess management time resolving issues;
Behaviour and conduct	Individuals or small teams in one or more locations behave or act such that catastrophic organisational damage occurs	Non-compliance with regulations / fines; employee work duplicated vs. knowledge shared; privacy / confidentiality breaches cause higher legal costs; fraud / collusion between staff and with 3rd parties; need to rebuild image / brand marketing increases costs;

Figure 27 Examples of impact from cultural disconnects

If costs can be minimized through eliminating the risks of adverse behaviour, margins can be improved. In 2016 OMS LLP., using the OMINDEX assessment system, conducted an analysis of Nestlé, which showed a rating of BBB-. This compared to a marketplace (S&P) rating at the much higher level of AA+. Based on this analysis, the OMR report suggested that Nestlé could, through enhanced approaches to strategic management of human capital, improve its margins by approximately 5%. This "gap" between traditional credit ratings and the OMINDEX demonstrates a risk / opportunity gap to risk and returns.

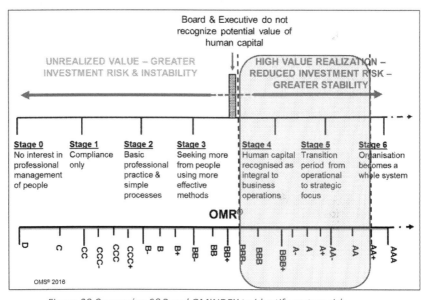

Figure 28 Comparing S&P and OMINDEX to identify system risk

This "rating gap" between AA+ and BBB- would suggest a risk in using the financially "biased" S&P rating as the only assessment of risk. There may be limited financial risk based on the earnings and balance sheet, together with the S&P analysts' evaluation of the company. However, the OMINDEX result would suggest that there is an opportunity to significantly enhance performance because its' "systemic health" appears lower.

The focus for Nestlé would be on "type 2" financial risks i.e., the buried costs" where there are expenses aggregated and buried within the existing business model that could be removed by an improvement in human centricity reflected by a higher OMINDEX rating.

9.4   Challenge 3: Building greater innovation and creativity

Even well-run organizations have the opportunity to improve; as an example, the OMS ratings of organizations considered leaders in the management of human capital score high, yet still have some level of opportunity / risk identified using the OMINDEX assessment, e.g., Toyota (A+), Costco (A) and Handelsbanken (A). Continued efforts by these organizations to focus on value creation, a holistic approach to complete system leadership, and human centric management could build competitive advantage.

In this area of financial risk, the problem is not one of surprise or buried costs, but a loss of opportunity to further enhance value in terms of OCRQ (increased Output, reduced Cost, increased Revenue, and increased Quality). Every day-to-day change that impacts these organizations carries "disruptive risk" that has an effect on its culture and can either diminish or enhance the effectiveness with which it deploys resources.

This third impact of risk, the problem of "lost opportunity" is potentially one of the most challenging. Traditional assessment of the organizations performance would probably place it in the mid or lower quartiles in its' industry. Management would be under pressure to improve performance and might well adopt approaches such as downsizing and layoffs, outsourcing, pressuring suppliers, and consolidating facilities. Yet in reality, the organization has the potential to grow and does not need to shrink. The actions being taken, while appearing to enhance short term performance may well reduce and deplete aspects of the culture that could add value. Where are the lost opportunities?

Strategic failure costs	Description of risk / opportunity
Limited continual improvement	Operational costs are not being continually reduced causing margin shrinkage; result is programs for cost reduction that often fail to remove the root cause of excess costs and lead to lowering of morale. The organization struggles to sustain a competitive advantage
Limited innovation	Related to the above; lip service paid to new ideas from employees; feedback is slow or non-existent and managers / leaders do not actively encourage employee innovation. Result is a maturing of capability and offerings which can often only be resolved through mergers / acquisitions or the "buying in" of patents and product / service opportunities
Limited ability to benefit from being "lean"	A lean organization is by definition one where there is very low levels of waste; however to "be lean" requires cooperation and collaboration across traditional functional organizational silos and a willingness of employees to take on more "caring and responsibility." Where people feel they are valued and recognized the probability is that lean initiatives will bring greater positive results
Responsiveness (market)	Organizations today seek to be "agile" and "responsive." These qualities come from employees who "care" and are willing to collaborate, cooperate and communicate; in short they are fully committed through what they do to the success of the business. A positive culture is one that creates this atmosphere; if these human qualities are not present the organization will not attain the capability.
Responsive (change)	Organizations need to be able to respond rapidly to changing markets and deploy their changes as rapidly as possible. Effective leadership which fully embraces its human capital and creates a culture of trust and commitment will develop a foundation for many rapid deployment of change than one where there is a lack of trust.

Figure 29 Elements of buried opportunity

In the table above we can see five examples; continual improvement is a known driver of competitive advantage for a company like Toyota, but it is widely known that many organizations try tools like suggestions schemes but fail to get "engagement."

Likewise, employees are not motivated to innovate or look for opportunities to eliminate every aspect of waste (to become "lean). They often will not go "the extra mile" for customers and clients; they may follow procedures, but it will not be a positive "moment of truth." Employees may also be reluctant to embrace change.

Strategic failure costs	Description of risk / opportunity
Responsive (regulatory)	For many organizations the regulatory framework within which they operate holds the power to support (speed up) or frustrate (slow down) certain business initiatives and changes. An organization that has open and transparent communications with regulators and which builds trust in its commitment to behaviour, compliance and responsiveness will likely be better supported and trusted by regulators when changes are needed.
Reputation loss	While purchase decisions are heavily financially based increasingly products are not differentiated, and the "ability to do business" with the company – i.e. the interactions between staff and clients becomes a key competitive edge. In this case a positive reputation through "staff who are knowledgeable and care" becomes a valuable asset in retaining clients and growing sales
Talent attraction	In many knowledge based companies, attraction and retention of human talent is a core requirement. Creating a reputation generated by existing employees as a "great place to work" will assist in the attraction of potential talent (especially in a competitive market where people have choices) as well as reducing the costs of hiring
Investor attraction	Investors are becoming increasingly concerned with organizational behaviour as it relates to the risk of their investment (both capital and returns). Organizations that develop sustain and communicate positive attributes that are seen to lower risk will have less challenge attracting investors and will possibly pay less of a financial risk premium for the money that they borrow.

Figure 30 More examples of limits to improvement

The list continues; interactions with regulators and others, which again can help support rapid changes, will be slower; the organization might lose out on opportunities to gain business because they do not" stand out" as a supplier of choice. They may also suffer from a shortage of talent; people may not seem them as a "preferred employer." Finally, investors may be less attracted, again as the organization does not differentiate itself. (Worse still, the organization may pay more for its borrowing costs?).

Constant reinforcement of the integrated and holistic approach to leadership and management is required to ensure that there is no negative "cultural drift." As discussed earlier, developing, and sustaining an effective culture never ends - it is an ongoing "way to operate." While "change" is a reality and is impacting almost every organization, the role of culture in adoption is critical to both the cost, and the speed of change. Both are critical competitive advantages.

9.5 Summary

For too many years organizations have given "lip service" to the phrase "people are our most important asset" yet often actual management of human capital as a strategic resource continues to focus on people as costs rather than investments.

Financial reporting often masks the impact that poor human capital management has on an organization's actual performance as well as its potential opportunity to reduce risk and enhance value creation. Understanding of the impact of human behaviour has been downplayed and often referred to as the "soft and fuzzy" side of management yet the growing importance of organizational culture is encouraging investors and leaders to take the issue of human behaviour and the optimization of human capital more seriously.

Because the impacts of poor or less than optimum approaches to human capital management are not clearly demonstrated through financial reporting, Investors, boards, and CEO's often fail to grasp the significance of a strategic focus around human-centric strategy and the benefits it can bring; often short term incentives add to the focus on short term performance that often exacerbates the challenge of shifting focus. Lack of performance and the desire for fast improvements may in fact worsen the strategic possibilities for real, underlying improvement.

There is a financial risk to less than optimum human-centric strategy; at worst this can expose the organization to higher operating costs including unplanned and unanticipated financial impacts, such as penalties and fines; for most organizations even at the medium and lower risk rankings there remains and opportunity to reduce hidden costs and enhance strategic competitive capability. At business grapples with the need for competitive advantage, transparency, and sustainability the adoption of additional measures that focus on whole system performance becomes a necessary imperative.

An effective corporate culture is the "enabling tool" for optimizing all resources necessary to enhance performance from an organizations business model,

Cost of Poor Culture: summary
• Poor culture often results in sub-optimization of organizational resources.
• Organizations with poor cultures tend to have higher risks related to behaviour that impact risk and enterprise sustainability.
• Poor culture can result in non-compliance and regulatory oversight that cost fines and penalties.
• Poor culture can allow individuals to act in a way damaging to the organization, its reputation and performance.
• Organizations with poor cultures are often unaware of the hidden operational costs and their impact on performance.
• Poor cultures negatively impact communication, cooperation, collaboration, innovation, and creativity.
• Good cultures enable rapid adjustment and change when required.
• Good cultures are the result of a strategic approach to the integrated optimization of all resources rather than the maximization of any single resource (e.g., financial performance).
• Depletion of a good culture can happen over time and only be realized once significant damage has been done to organizational capacity and competitiveness.
• Annual audits and audit reports, including MD&A (Management Discussion and Analysis) give limited insight into risk related to culture.
• Broad based performance reporting is needed to assess optimization of resources other than financial.

Cost of Poor Culture: Checklist
• Is there a defined "crucible culture" that forms a key aspect of organizational strategy?
• Is there a culture of trust and openness that allows a healthy culture to flourish and enhance performance?
• Does the Board give equal importance to cultural and behavioural strategy, goals, and measurement as to financial performance?
• Is the CEO measured on culture and behaviour equally to their financial performance?
• Has the organization developed a clear understanding and implemented the link between risks, internal controls, and behaviours?
• Has the organization developed a clear understanding of performance enabling behaviours?
• Have these behaviours been linked to organizational outcomes linked to competitive advantage and growth?
• Has the organization suffered any "surprises" and if so, were these investigated relative to culture?
• Are all the employees actively engaged in "constructive criticism" of the organizational operations and do their ideas contribute significantly to growth and improvement?
• Has the organization ever conducted a "Cost of Poor Culture" assessment and review to determine the financial impact of their existing culture?

10 Appendix

The appendix contains a number of forms, list and documents that have been developed over the years in working with clients to assist in the development of aspects related to organizational culture. These may be utilized as examples and templates if they can help an organization on its "cultural journey." The following is a summary:

Pre-survey

 An EduVision Inc. Knowledge Service	Culture Survey
Company / Client	
Stage:	Preliminary Planning

Score as follows: Strongly agree (5), Agree (4), Neutral (3), Disagree (2) Strongly Disagree (1)

#	Question	5	4	3	2	1
1	Our organization has a clear purpose					
2	I understand how my job supports our purpose					
3	Our company has clear behavioural values					
4	I am fairly compensated for my work					
5	I have clear direction for my work					
6	I have the tools / equipment for my work					
7	Workloads are usually reasonable					
8	Our stated values guide decision making					
9	I am valued for my contribution					
10	I am trusted to perform my work					
11	Internal communications are effective					
12	Collaboration is supported					
13	I am treated fairly by the organization					
14	Employee suggestions are encouraged					
15	People cooperate in our organization					
16	People have the opportunity to develop					
17	Learning and development are encouraged					
18	I trust my supervisor					
19	This organization operates ethically					
20	Stress is well managed in our workplace					
	Total results					

This example has 20 questions that might be asked during the development of the "where are we now?" stage of developing culture. The answers will provide a basis for discussion on the foundations of developing values. It can also be used during development. Maximum score would be 100, 20 the lowest. Most organizations, with "real answers" would probably score 50% - 60%.

Balance / Bias survey

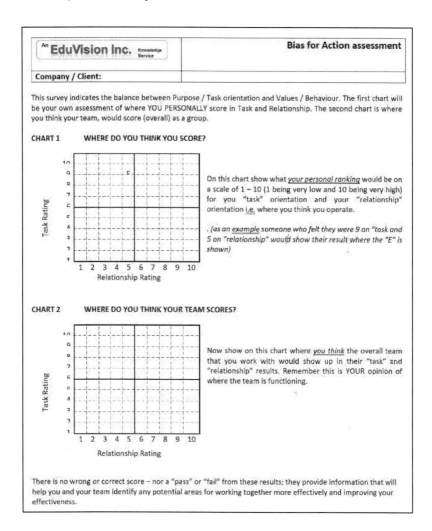

This survey is an optional approach that may help organizations understand the level (or lack of) balance between focusing on Purpose and Task, versus the importance given to behaviour - how "we do things around here." This sometimes understand the bias that has built over time to "just get the job done" and not worry about behaviour.

How to know / measure development

An EduVision Inc. Knowledge Service	Value Development
Company / Client:	

Value	Challenge	Ideas for assessment criteria
Ensure respect for people's dignity and integrity	How to measure	Employee survey by job position # of HR Supervisory actions / problems Results from exit interviews Results from employee reviews
Create and maintain a collaborative work environment	How to measure	Employee survey Employee suggestions / submitted / implemented # self managed work teams # CI teams in place (join with measure of results) Results from exit interviews Results from employee reviews
Embrace innovation	Link to technology strategy	# suggestions / ideas implemented Savings from improvement suggestions # new services / products introduced % of revenue from products / services not in place 3 years or more previous Spending on development (R&D / application) # ideas identified by supplier partner network Patents successfully registered

Often a key challenge as ideas for values develop is how to "operationalize" these statements - "how would we know?" This type of worksheet for collecting ideas and brainstorming can be helpful.

Is / Is not Operational Discussion

An EduVision Inc. Knowledge Service	Operational Values Development Is / Is Not Discussion
Company / Client:	
Values statements version dated:	

To be recognized as a supplier of high quality products and services.	
This Means ("Is" statement)	**This is not...**
❑ To have and achieve a policy of zero defects and compliance with customer specifications ❑ To achieve 100% on time delivery ❑ To provide the employees with the leadership, tools, equipment and authority to achieve this Value ❑ Using achievement of this goal to leverage our business in the marketplace and with our customers ❑ Strongly encourage our plants to strive for a level of customer satisfaction that drives preferred relationships ❑ To recognize and reward the employees for excellence in quality, delivery and client satisfaction. ❑ To employ a systematic approach to proactively evaluate root causes of quality / delivery problems to ensure that corrective actions are taken ❑ To apply the principle of benchmarking as a cornerstone to identify best practise that drives continues improvement ❑ To proactively solve customer problems ❑ Use cross functional teams that work to focus on quality improvements as a way to build increased competitive advantage with the customer ❑ Take a honest approach to the management of quality	❑ Taking a zero tolerance approach to both these targets with Management ❑ Sacrificing the Value in order to meet cost budgets or delivery schedules ❑ Telling the customer that he / she is wrong

This is another example of the worksheet included in the test that looks at an alternative value - in this case relative to its relationships with clients. Probably would be linked to brand and reputation.

Leaders commitment

An EduVision Inc. Knowledge Service						Leadership Values Commitment Development Worksheet
Company / Client:						
Name:						

Value as stated

Strongly disagree
Disagree
Neutral - Neither agree or disagree
Agree
Strongly Agree

	5	4	3	2	1	Comments
I understand what this value means						
As a manager I choose this value freely						
I publicly affirm this value						
I prize and cherish this value						
I act on this value consistently						
I can measure how well I am doing						
This value is demonstrated by others						
My business plan includes this value						

Discussion, comments notes, ideas on measurements

This is an additional and expanded example of the discussion with people in leadership positions about their comfort with the organizational values. Note that there are added questions related to "self-assessment."

Personal self-assessment for leaders

An EduVision Inc. Knowledge Service	Self-assessment
Company / Client:	
Individual and team / department:	

Scoring Strongly agree (5), Agree (4), Neutral (3), Disagree (2), Strongly disagree (1).

#	Self-assessment question	1	2	3	4	5
1	I try to understand what others are saying					
2	I try to understand what others are feeling					
3	I try to bring us back on topic, over talkative people in the group					
4	I try and encourage reluctant people to speak up					
5	At times, I change roles in the group to help the group accomplish our objectives for the session					
6	I try to help the group evaluate all the information we have at our disposal so that a consensus is more possible than a compromise					
7	My comments sometimes sidetrack the conversation					
8	I sometimes interrupt others so they cannot finish their thoughts, ideas or provide needed information					
9	I tend to dominate the group's discussion					
10	I sometimes push the group too fast to some definite solution, commitment, or acceptance of information					
11	I acknowledge others for their contribution to the discussion					
12	I sometimes minimize the feelings of other team members					
13	At times I feel myself holding back information					
14	I express my thoughts and feelings without hesitation					
15	I communicate in a way that builds trust					
16	I ask for clarification when I do not understand what someone says					
17	I show concern when a fellow team member is having difficulty					
18	When I strongly disagree with someone, I express it in a respectful manner					
19	I actively seek to learn from other team members					
20	When working on a project, I seek out different ideas and opinions					

Totals					

Average score	

Self-assessment is a critical skill for anyone in a leadership position. Only through a high level of self awareness can the manager be open to changes in their behaviour that supports or detracts from the desired culture. This type of tool can help the thinking; it can also be used as a discussion with the person's team.

11 Bibliography

Becker, Brian. E., Huselid, Mark. A., Ulrich, F. Dave. The HR Scorecard," 2001, Harvard Business Press.

Blanchard, Ken., O'Connor, Michael., "Managing by Values."1997, Berrett-Koehler

Campanella, Jack., "Principles of Quality Costs,3rd edition"1999, Quality Press, ASQ

Carter, Jimmy., "Our Endangered Values," 2005, Simon & Schuster

Cohen, Ben., Warwick, Mal., "Values Driven Business," 2006, Berrett-Koehler

Collins, Jim., "How the Mighty Fall," 2009, Harper Collins

Conger, Jay. A., Tichy, Noel. M., Schein, Edgar. H., Champy, James. A., Kets de Vries, Manfred. F.R., "Organization 21C"2002, Financial Times, Prentice Hall

Crosby, Phil., "Quality is Free,", Signet, 1979.

Fitz-enz, Jac., "The ROI of Human Capital,"2000, AMACOM

Lev, Baruch., Gu, Feng., "The End of Accounting." 2016, Wiley

Gleeson-White, Jane., "Six Capitals: The Revolution Capitalism has to have - of can accountants save the planet." 2014, Allen & Unwin

Kaplan, Robert. S., Norton, David. P., "The Balanced Scorecard," 1996, Harvard Business Review Press

Kaplan, Robert. S., Norton, David. P., "Alignment," 2006, Harvard Business School Publishing

Kearns. P., Woollard, Stuart., "The Mature Corporation," 2019, Cambridge Scholars Press

Liker, Jeffrey. K., "Toyota Under Fire: How Toyota faced the challenges of the recall and came out stronger." 2011 McGraw Hill

Liker, Jeffrey. K., "The Toyota Way." 2004, McGraw Hill

Liker, Jeffrey. K., Hoseus, Michael., "Toyota Culture: The Heart and Soul of the Toyota Wat." 2008, McGraw Hill

Liker, Jeffrey. K., Meier, David. P., "Toyota Talent; Developing Your People the Toyota Way." 2007, McGraw Hill

Magee, David., "How Toyota Became #1." 2007 Portfolio

Nayar, Vineet., "Employees First, Customers Second,"2010, Harvard Business Press

Rother, Mike., "Toyota Kata." 2010, McGraw Hill

Schmidt, Eric., Rosenberg, Jonathan., "How Google Works," 2014, Hachette Book Group Ltd.

Shepherd, Nick. A., "Governance, Accountability and Sustainable Development: An agenda for the 21st Century." 2005, Thompson Carswell Canada

Stewart, Tom., "Intellectual Capital: The New Wealth of Nations" Currency Doubleday, 1997,

Wallis, Jim., "Rediscovering Values," 2010, Simon & Schuster

Weiss, David. S., "High Performance HR," 2000, John Wile

NICK A. SHEPHERD
FCPA, FCGA, FCCA, FCMC,

Nick has over 50 years of varied work experience including senior general management and finance roles. From 1989 to 2017 he ran his own management consulting and professional development company. Currently he is officially retired but still spends time on research and writing. Nick currently focuses his efforts in the areas of organizational sustainability, human capital, and integrated reporting. Nick has experience working in, and with private family business, public corporations, and governments and NPO's. Nick is currently a Director and Council member of the UK based Maturity Institute.

As a management consultant and facilitator, Nick designed and presented many professional development workshops internationally, and across Canada. Nick was also part-time faculty member at Grenoble Graduate School of Business (GGSB) where he taught modules on Mergers and Acquisitions and Management Consulting; Nick also lectured at McMaster / DeGroote on ethics. Nick led the Professional Standards Committee of the International Council of Management Consultants in developing the competency model that now forms the basis of CMC certification in over 50 global CMC Institutes. In 2007 Nick received the President's Award for Education from the Certified General Accountants of British Columbia. Nick's consulting work included both public and private sector clients in many countries including Canada, the US, the UK, the Caribbean, South Africa, Kazakhstan, Kyrgyzstan, Uzbekistan, and Jordan.

Nick joined CPA Ontario as a Fellow in 2014 following the merger of accounting bodies. Prior to that Nick was a CGA for over 35 years obtaining his Fellowship in 2009. Nick is a Fellow of the Chartered Association of Certified Accountants (FCCA UK), and a Fellow of the Institute of Certified Management Consultants of Ontario (FCMC – Honour Roll), and Past President of the Institute. Nick is Past Chair of the National Certification Committee for all Institutes of Management Consulting across Canada, and Past Chair of the Professional Standards Committee of the International Council of Management Consulting Institutes (ICMCI). He served as one of four trustees for Canada at the International level (ICMCI). Nick has also been a member of Mensa for many years.

Nick is co-author of "Reflective Leaders and High Performing Organizations" written in 2012 with Dr. Peter Smyth. Nick also wrote "Governance, Accountability and Sustainable Development" in 2005, that deals with Governance issues for the 21st century, and the "Controllers Handbook" (now in its 2nd edition) – these books add to a number of other books and articles that Nick has authored, including "Values and Ethics: From Inception to Practice," "The Evolution of Accountability – Sustainability Reporting for Accountants," "Unrecognized Intangible Assets: Identification, Management and Reporting" and "The Human Aspects of Cost Control." Nick also developed several Ethics courses for accountants and consultants nationally and internationally.

Contact Nick at nick@eduvision.ca

Manufactured by Amazon.ca
Bolton, ON